JAPANESE
CAR

Marco Ruiz

JAPANESE CAR

Illustrations by Amedeo Gigli

Portland House

New York

The Publisher would like to thank the public relations departments
of Japanese automobile companies
for kindly supplying textual and photographic material.

This 1986 edition
published by Portland House
distributed by Crown Publishers, Inc.,
225 Park Avenue South,
New York, New York 10003

Conceived by Enzo Angelucci

Created by Adriano Zannino
Editorial assistant Serenella Genoese Zerbi
Editor Maria Luisa Ficarra, Victoria Lee
Translated from the Italian by James Ramsay and Valerie Palmer

ISBN 0-517-61777-3

Colour separation SEBI srl, Milan
Typesetting Tipocrom srl, Rome

Printed in Italy by SAGDOS S.p.A., Milan

CONTENTS

INTRODUCTION

The ascent of the Japanese automobile can be described as a happy combination of social, economic, commercial and technical factors skillfully orchestrated by a state which has engineered its development to great effect, by precise and capable choices of timing and method.

At the outset was a challenge, only realized after World War II: to focus on a national industry which was still in its infancy, while keeping the products and capital of the American industrial giants at bay. Hence the astute decision to proceed with reconstruction of the country, restricting the local consumption with production hinged almost exclusively on industrial vehicles. Not until the sixties was the go-ahead given for a period of frenzied growth in private motoring, the necessary know-how in terms of engineering and design being imported from the West. As a result, by the time of the oil crisis in the following decade, a product was already available which was capable of responding to the new energy requirements and thus able to take its place successfully on international markets. Such a "violent" process of international expansion inevitably provoked protectionist reactions from those countries whose automobile industries were most threatened. Hence the radical change in strategy in the eighties, with a voluntary or "agreed" restriction of exports and a commercial aggressivity which the constant revaluation of the yen no longer permitted to be based on favorable prices alone. From a technical viewpoint, the result has been a leap in quality for a product which has become essentially avantgarde and attractive, while in commercial terms the massive exportation of capital to open production facilities on the "enemy's," own doorstep has changed the face of the Japanese invasion, which has only partially been offset by a cautious opening of their domestic market to imports. All in all, it has been a development coldly and rationally determined, devoid of those "heroic" pioneering impulses which characterized the growth of the Western industry. Surprisingly, however, the evidence of a passion long and artificially sacrificed is seen in the first rudimentary attempts at automobile production which inspired Japan too at the beginning of the century, just as involvement in sport at the highest levels has succeeded in giving its international growth a more emotional element. This book is the first attempt to retrace the different lines of development of an industrial phenomenon without precedent, which has made Japan a genuine protagonist of that "civilization of the automobile" which today represents one of the few areas in which such diverse traditions and mentalities can genuinely unite.

THE DAWNING
OF
JAPANESE MOTORIZATION

The inhabitants of the small, quiet fishing port of Shimoda, south of Tokyo, must have experienced a rude awakening at the sight of Admiral Matthew Perry's «black ships» anchored off their coast in the year 1853. After two and a half centuries of feudalism and commercial isolation, the treaty which the American commodore forced the Japanese authorities to agree to a year later meant the return of Japan to the international community, with the reopening of its ports. Radical changes in the country's social and economic structures followed. Over the long and difficult Meiji Restoration period, the old feudal system gradually gave way to an economy based on private ownership of land and (to a lesser extent) commercial exchange. Other Western powers followed the United States. Drawn by Japan's enormous gold reserves, they negotiated highly profitable agreements, selling heavy industrial produce to a country whose only exports were tea, raw silk and a few semi-worked goods. Japanese imports thus rocketed, while the nation's young industries (textile related) were powerless against the «rigged» prices at which foreign goods were selling. State intervention was needed to cope with a situation in which production initiatives at home were thus constantly undermined (this was to be so especially in the car industry). Alternatively, Japanese manufacturers had to confine themselves to areas where they would not be in competition with overseas companies (e.g. light manufacturing industries). To direct the capital of Japan's first businessmen, the Meiji government concentrated on creating a banking system capable of supplying the requisite finance. At the same time trade was encouraged by a tax system based on land-taxes, which permitted vast accumulation of profits and together with a tendency of concentration on new Japanese companies led to the *zaibatsu*: powerful industrial cartels, controlling monopolies, able to recruit extremely cheap labor from the overpopulated rural villages. Japan thus gradually achieved greater negotiating muscle in its dealings with the West, introducing its own autonomous customs system in 1911. Meanwhile, the government had discouraged foreign investment since 1870, thereby insuring that the nation's growth was not reliant on such external interests. This policy had been urged by the new capitalist class, and resulted for instance in operations such as the large loan made to Mitsubishi in 1875 for the recovery of the Tokyo-Shanghai trade route from American Pacific. This tradition of independent development was never to be abandoned, except when absolutely necessary. Importation of foreign «know-how» was, however, encouraged through the purchase of Western technology (albeit at a high price).

Torao Yamaba and his family in the steam-driven car built by him in 1904.

The 8 hp twin-cylinder produced by Tokyo Kunisue Automobile Works in 1910.

The first Takuri Type 3 of 1907, the first true Japanese automobile.

The first cars

The first recorded Japanese-made motor vehicle was a steam car built in 1904 by Torao Yamaba. It had a 2-cylinder engine developing about 25 hp. Built to carry the extensive Yamaba family, it had ten seats and was generously proportioned, being some 14.7 ft (4.5 m) long and 4.5 ft (1.4 m) wide. It had chain-drive. However, the necessary technology to construct a gasoline fueled motor was already available, since gasoline engines (both 2- and 4-cylinder, two- and four-stroke, air- or water-cooled) for stationary use had been imported and even produced in Japan for some time. The first real Japanese car thus dates from 1907, with the Takuri, of which a dozen were built in all — a considerable number for its time. It was produced by the enterprising Automobile Trading Co., which in 1902 had already assembled a 2-cylinder (12 hp) steam car with imported components. The owner, Shintaro Yoshida, who had gained experience of the car business in the United States, was aided in producing the Takuri by Komanosuke Uchiyama, the first professional car designer. A number of European cars provided the basis of the design, especially the Darracq and Laurin & Klement, which Prince Arisugawa (who was financing the venture) had previously imported through Yoshida's trading company. Before the final version was built, at the Tokyo Automobile Works, there were two prototypes (Takuri Type 1 and Type 2). The Type 3 had a twin-cylinder horizontally-opposed engine imported from the United States. It had a displacement of 1,850 cc, developing 12 hp. With cone clutch transmission, it had two gears and twin chain-drive. The steel chassis had box-type ladder frame, and the suspension was semi-elliptic leafsprings on all four wheels. The magnificent bodywork had a basic wooden structure, and there were four luxurious leather seats. The Takuri was a rugged vehicle, built with contemporary road conditions in mind (for there was motorized traffic only in certain large cities). The financial difficulties of producing such innovative vehicles, however, persuaded Yoshida to return to exclusively commercial activity. Car production was only taken up again in 1910, by the Tokyo Kunisue Automobile Works, which built a small but strong four-seater convertible (2-cylinder, water-cooled, approx. 8 hp at 1,800 rpm). Then in 1911, together with the Tokyo Motor Vehicle Works, Kunisue built

Nevertheless, by 1900 the number of factory employees was still under half a million, and of the 7,000 industrial businesses throughout Japan, 4,150 were textile related, and the low level of technology is indicated by the fact that of these only 2,388 were mechanized. Almost all machinery was imported up until 1910 and although by the 1930s Japan was self-sufficient in this area, it still remained an essentially agricultural society.

Industrialization received government encouragement particularly after the successful war against Russia (1905), when it became clear, with the adoption of Western-style colonialist policies in Asia, that Japan needed an adequate military force. In 1910 studies of a whole range of military motor vehicles were made, their first use probably being in 1914, in World War I, in the Tsingtao offensive. Heavy industry was thus grafted by the government on a Japan that was not yet ready to produce its own. It is extraordinary when one thinks how in 1910 when the world's first «all big gun» battleship, the «Satsuma,» was built, Japan had not managed to produce a single textile machine. In the early decades of the present century, therefore, Japan was a Third World country in relation to the West, and a capitalist power in relation to the developing countries of Asia. Hence, while the car industry flourished in Europe and mass production started in the United States (in 1910 the Olds Motor Vehicle Co. built 181,000 Curved Dash cars), the automobile sector in Japan remained a purely marginal interest of the rich middle class, with a few cars imported as luxury toys from the West, and very few and far between, home-produced Japanese models. On the narrow, bad conditioned roads of a country where the traditional man-drawn *rikisha* and *daihachiguruma* were still in use, these first motor vehicles were unpopular, and hardly seemed to herald the growth of an industry that was to take the whole world by surprise. Virtually no significant developments were to occur, indeed, until the great earthquake of 1923.

Only a few models were built of this «Tokyo» car of 1911, which was the first Japanese 4-cylinder.

a luxury sedan, the first Japanese car to have a 4-cylinder engine.

It was water-cooled, with magneto ignition, an L-head, approximately 1.3 liters; 16-18 hp at 1,800 rpm. It had a 3-speed transmission with cardan-shaft drive. This model was not produced on any commercially significant scale. By 1912 the small circle of Japanese car makers had probably produced fewer than 50 passenger cars in all. Thereafter new ventures started, and car manufacture became more of an industry, with production lines appearing. One of the most important of these ventures was that embarked on by Masujiro Hashimoto who, after gaining experience and expertise working with engineering firms in the United States, founded the Kwaishinsha Motor Car Co. in 1911. His cars were given the name DAT, and the most historic model was the 41, built in 1916, the forerunner of the Datsun. It was a small 1.5-liter, L-head, water-cooled sedan (15.8 hp), available in either open or closed versions. With multidisc clutch it had 4-speed gears, a drive shaft and hypoid bevel. Another big name in this early phase of the Japanese car industry was the Osaka based Jitsuyo Jidosha Co., which in 1919 brought out the se-

The DAT 41 of 1916 had 4-cylinder water-cooled engine, L-head, delivering 15.8 hp, and was available in either open or closed versions. It was the forerunner of the Datsun.

The Mitsubishi «Model A» project of 1917, small numbers of which were built up to 1921, was inspired by the Fiat Zero made in Italy in 1912.

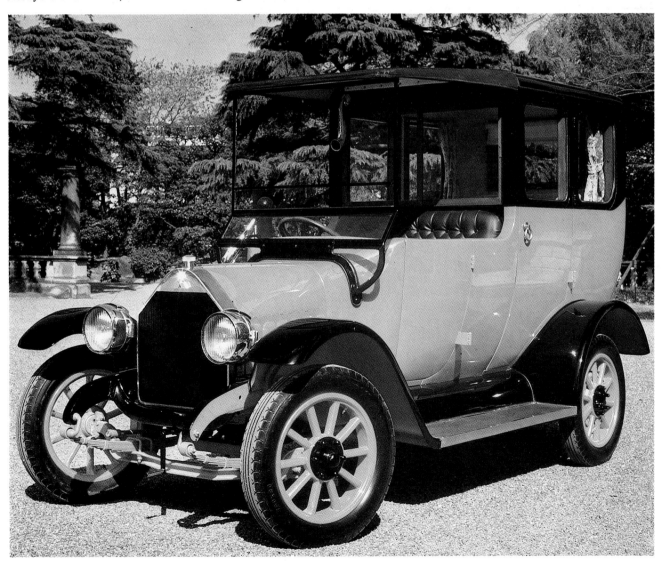

dan and sports models of the Lila, the first Japanese car designed with the possibility of mass production in mind. It was deliberately straightforward to assemble, and the plain body, mounted on a rail-frame, had the minimum of aesthetic and functional elements. Also the more luxurious Gorham came out, but met with no market success. After the 1923 earthquake Kwaishinsha and Jitsuyo joined forces, to form (after a number of changes) the Nissan company. Meanwhile in 1916 the shipbuilders Ishikawajima entered the car sector in collaboration with another Japanese company, the Tokyo Gas and Electric Industrial Co. Two years later an agreement was made with the English firm Wolseley, and in 1922 there appeared the first Wolseley car to be built under license entirely in Japan.

Hakuyosha Co. (Tokyo) came closest to mass production

at this time with the Otomo, brought out in 1924. Designed by J. Toyokawa (also American-trained), some 150 Otomos were built per annum throughout the twenties, with a few tentative exports to China. To complete the picture of this gestation period of the Japanese car industry, there was also the Ohta company, founded in Tokyo in 1912, which was to remain in business until the fifties. All these early forays into car production were financed by limited «venture capital» investments, while the *zaibatsus'* first steps into private motorization were taken by Mitsubishi, who produced a limited number of Model A cars between 1917 and 1921.

The infancy of the Japanese car industry

It was only as the 1920s approached that the Japanese government began to take an interest in car manufacture and to give it some financial support. A considerable boost was given by the law passed in 1918 concerning subsidies to manufacturers of military vehicles, which gave the whole sector a decidedly militarized tone. There was thus naturally greater production of industrial vehicles (an emphasis that only changed after World War II). Kwaishinsha and Tokyo Gas Denki collaborated to produce considerable numbers of trucks, and Ishikawajima and others

The American William R. Gorham, having founded an aeronautical company in Japan in 1918 which failed immediately, devoted himself to the construction of trucks and three-wheeled vehicles, which were produced by Jitsuyo Jidosha Co. The latter built the Lila series, of which we see two examples, from 1923 (left) and 1926 (below).

After having built a few Ales prototypes between 1920 and 1921 engineer Junya Toyokawa began a series production of the Otomo in 1924 (left). A 944 cc 4-cylinder air-cooled engine with 3-gear transmission.
The 1936 Otha phaeton (right) was one of the first examples of original good Japanese design.

Inspired by the English Austin Seven of 1922, the first Datson produced on 1931 (above) had a 495 cc 4-cylinder with side-valve engine. In 1932 with Datsun as its modified name, the displacement was increased to 744 cc. On the right is the 1935 model Type 14 Roadster.

were also engaged in the same area, but as far as civilian motor vehicles were concerned, imports were still greater than home production: in 1923 out of 12,700 motor vehicles in Japan, fewer than 1,000 were made in the country. The first real stimulus to car production was caused by the horrific earthquake that shook Tokyo and Yokohama, claiming hundreds of thousands of victims, in 1923. The quakes destroyed both the railway and the urban tramway systems, thus creating immediate problems for the supply of aid and longer term difficulties of communication. Suddenly the authorities were made to realize the importance of motor vehicles, and the first thing they did

The DA model (482 cc) presented in 1931 was the first vehicle produced under Mazda trade-mark.

was to order a thousand buses from the United States, to restore transport within the relevant cities. Demand for trucks became ever greater, especially as the rebuilding of the country's capital got under way. However, the home automobile industry, undeveloped as it had been, was based largely in the Kanto region which had been hardest hit by the earthquake, and had thus been almost totally wiped out.

It was to the two great American companies, General Motors and Ford, that Japan had to turn. Imports, which in 1923 had numbered 1,938, shot up to 4,063 in 1924, and remained on a similar scale for the whole decade. This demand firmly established these American manufacturers in Japan, and rather than continue the huge export process, they set up local assembly plants: thus the Japan Ford Motor Co. appeared in Yokohama in 1925, followed two years later by the Japan General Motors Co. in Osaka. In 1929, of the approximative 35,000 vehicles absorbed onto the Japanese market, 29,388 had been assembled locally. Imports of ready assembled vehicles that year numbered 5,018, while Japanese built models sold a mere 437. Among the bigger of these Japanese companies, Hakuyosha went out of business in the face of American competition in 1927. Political interest in car production slowly grew, however, albeit primarily with war needs in mind, as evidenced clearly at the invasion of Manchuria in 1931, after which Japanese heavy industry was encouraged to expand vigorously. The military state of affairs made it increasingly vital for the country to develop its own industry and to reduce imports of foreign vehicles, thereby correcting a situation of dangerous economic dependence and encouraging growth of a domestic car industry — a growth and confidence that would then spread to the rest of Japanese industry. Some co-ordination of effort was needed. However, throughout the 1920s a large number of small firms had appeared which now fragmented production, presenting a grave risk to an economy already weakened by the crisis of 1929. Through clever subsidies the government encouraged industrial concentration, and hence the formation of new powerful *zaibatsu*, bound both financially and politically to the government, and there-

fore forming a reliable source of supply for the war effort of the thirties, as the war with China gradually escalated. This change in government attitude bore immediate fruit, with the creation of Nissan in 1934: a merger of Jitsuyo and DAT, to give a production capacity of 20,000 vehicles per year. Meanwhile in 1933 Toyota had entered the arena, with one million yen behind it. The nation's large capital pools had thus finally been fed into the car sector, the one area of Japanese industry that had evolved entirely on foreign capital. The collaboration between the government and the large car companies became very close, as when the standard specifications for trucks (1.5- and 2-ton) and consequently for buses were set for military use. Models produced in a joint-venture between a number of companies after 1934 were termed Isuzu. Yet progress was restricted, and military considerations led the government to act more decisively against foreign products, with the 1936 Motorcar Manufacturing Enterprise Law which effectively ended the American companies' activity. Among other things companies in the car sector had to have government authorization and a least half of the capital, of the shareholders and of the directors had to be Japanese. Such companies had furthermore to comply with directives issued by the military authorities. Only Toyota, Nissan and Isuzu were permitted to remain in business by the terms of this legislation. Japan Ford and Japan GM had first to cut production drastically, and then eventually to close after the 1937 Chinese episode. Cars were of course considered less important than industrial vehicles: the production records for 1936 give 5,004 trucks and buses, 6,335 «small vehicles» (for sundry purposes), and only 847 cars. Far and away the most popular form of transport were three-wheeled vehicles (almost all trucks), of which 12,840 were made that year. In 1937 this figure rose to 15,000. Three-wheeled vehicles had been introduced by Hatsudoki Seizo (the future Daihatsu) in 1930, with Toyo Kogyo producing the Mazda truck one year later. For some time already, car companies had been considering the need for a small, rugged car quite unlike the large American models, but tailored to popular demand. Development was somewhat slow, however, due both to lack of specific financing and to the unreadiness of the market. Nevertheless, various models, now forgotten, were brought out during the twenties. The first to achieve any real success was the 1931 Datson developed from the DAT 41 (only later was the name changed to Datsun — now a standard name for any economy car). This car was mentioned in a leading article in the London *Times* as another threat to British industry, similar to that posed by Japanese textile products. Production of civilian cars was deliberately restricted by the Japanese government, however, as the country was kept relatively closed to private consumption, and the road network remained completely inadequate (two factors which combined to form a solid protectionist barrier against foreign cars). Imported vehicles became less and less competitive against home produced cars specifically designed for these difficult driving conditions, even though the Japanese products were small and spartan.

By December 1941, on the eve of the Pacific War, annual production had reached 46,498, of which more than half

Taken from the American Graham-Paige, the Nissan Type 70 sedan, shown above in the Special version, was introduced in 1937.

The A-1 model (below) was the first car developed by Toyota in 1935. It had a displacement of 3.4-liter with 6 cylinders and a rating of 62 hp.

was for military use. When it came to the supply of raw materials and marketing, the car industry was directly under government control. With the dramatic change in the war situation in 1942, the need to strengthen the air force meant a gradual decline in truck production. The Toyota and Nissan factories turned largely to making aircraft engines, while on the technical side, both companies researched alternative types of engine (e.g. diesel fueled), of which the post-war civilian industry was to reap the benefits despite a certain technological standstill following the break of contact with the West. To sum up, therefore, cars had never figured prominently in Japanese industrial policy up to this point, and involvement in car production (first with experimental models, then on a limited series production) had always been through groups already established in other areas of industry diversifying their activity. For instance, Mitsubishi and Tobata (Nissan) were already powerful holding companies with interests in a variety of fields; Toyota and Suzuki had grown up in the textile world, and Toyo Kogyo had dealt in cork products. A far cry from the situation in the West.

The postwar reconstruction

At the end of the war the Japanese car industry found itself in a very precarious position. Production capacity had been reduced to a mere 1,500 due to the changeover to munitions during the war and the devastation of the latter stages. Nominally 110,000 vehicles (cars, commercial vehicles and buses) were in circulation, but probably only 80,000 at the most were in proper working condition, given their age and the lack of spare parts. The Japanese economy was in the hands of the SCAP (Supreme Commander for the Allied Powers), which was in practice run by the United States alone, under the direction of General MacArthur. This American control of the Japanese economy did not alter the prewar political structures, thus encouraging continuity advantageous to the industrial power-holders. Therefore when the United States resolved to do away with the *zaibatsu* (as being dangerous, militaristic monopolies), the operation was essentially planned by the Japanese industrialists themselves, closely linked economically as they were both to the Japanese political authorities and to numerous American companies. Furthermore the reform program had no effect on the banking and credit system, which was the real key to the power of the *zaibatsu*. Soon the USA changed their mind, sensing that a reconstruction of Japanese industry under their strict control would give them a valuable ally in an area of great strategic importance. A program of decentralization of production was continued until 1948, however, and this naturally also affected the car industry. The Fuji Sangyo group, for example, was split into 12 independent companies, six of which then reunited some years later to form the Fuji Heavy Industries. By a similar process Tachikawa Aircraft gave birth to Prince Motor. Back in 1942, Hino had already left the Tokyo Jidosha group which produced Isuzu vehicles, to form its own independent business. Car production recommenced according to the rigid regulations issued by SCAP. On September 25

The first truck produced by Toyota after the war was the «SB», taken from the SA car series. Between April 1947 and 1952, 12,800 of them were built.

1945, after US military vehicles had coped with the immediate needs of civilian transport, authorization was given for the construction of 1,500 trucks. This marked the beginning of the industry's revival.

Then in June 1947 production of 300 cars (below 1,500 cc) annually was permitted. In 1948 the number of vehicles on the roads rose to 181,000, exceeding the last prewar (1940) figure of 152,000 for the first time. The following year, when car production was allowed full rein, Japanese-made vehicles totaled 28,700, bringing the grand total of vehicles on the roads to over 200,000. Of these however in February 1950 88% were ten years old, or older.

Japan's reviving motor industry at first concentrated on trucks, especially three-wheelers. Nevertheless, it was not until 1953 that vehicle production (49,800 that year) exceeded the total for 1941. Demand and production in the car sector were slowed by a number of causes. Firstly, people's average purchasing power, which was low already, was further diminished by heavy taxes (between 20 and 50% of the price). Secondly, there was strong competition in the form of second-hand cars sold by US occupation personnel, which were exempt from the heavy customs duties on new imported cars. There thus developed a market in new Western cars sold in Japan as used cars. In 1953 12,503 cars were bought from US personnel, as opposed to 8,789 put on the market by Japanese companies. Japan's economic recovery was such as to enable more people to buy cars, but US models were both unpractical and problematic (in terms of servicing and spares), and the Japanese manufacturers were still not yet sufficiently developed, and so private car ownership did not increase quickly. Even the war in Korea (one of the major factors in Japan's economic recovery) further contributed to the bias towards industrial vehicle production, with large orders put in by the USA. At the political level there was also lively debate over how to boost the country's car industry. Hisato Ichimada, governor of the Bank of Japan, who was considered the fount of all economic wisdom in the country at the time, was convinced that private car ownership could best be encouraged by importing technologically advanced cars at low cost from USA and Europe. While in the United States the Ford Model T had topped four million sales by 1920, Japanese cars were still hybrids evolved from commercial vehicles, and decidedly unglamorous to look at. There were a good 40 years of progress to catch up on. The Transport Minister himself proposed starting an import policy. Very soon, however, the traditional Japanese belief that anything ought to be able to be produced at home surfaced again. The Minister for Industry and International Trade («MITI») declared that it was vital for the national economy that a sound car manufacturing industry be developed, and that it would take only a few years to acquire the advanced technology being used in the West. This was in 1952, and over the next two years a series of measures were introduced which in practice ended imports into Japan.

The apprentice years

The Japanese motor industry was thus committed to doing it alone. Acts were passed to encourage and support it: for instance, substantial financial aid was available to build low cc cars, and the purchase tax on such cars was reduced. At the same time the conditions of the sale of «used» imported cars were made more stringent, and government departments were obliged to use only home produced vehicles. More and more Nissan and Toyota taxis appeared in the large cities, replacing the old Fords and Chevrolets. Yet the car industry, and indeed Japanese industries in all sectors, faced a socio-economic situation that was hardly very favorable.

For a start, demand for cars was still low due to general lack of purchasing power among a population coping with the effects of post-war recession and galoping inflation. Most cars on the roads before the fifties were either taxis or rented cars. A few were owned privately by state officials and industrialists, or sometimes by doctors, who would visit homes by car. Such a market was not likely to create an immediate expansion of production. The in-

The Datsun DX Sedan of 1951 had an 860 cc 4-cylinder engine with lateral valves, derived from the old 722 cc. The power was 20 hp at 3,600 rpm.

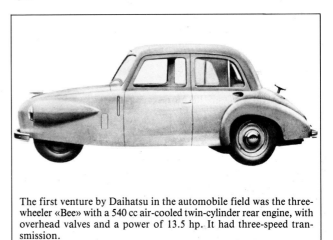

The first venture by Daihatsu in the automobile field was the three-wheeler «Bee» with a 540 cc air-cooled twin-cylinder rear engine, with overhead valves and a power of 13.5 hp. It had three-speed transmission.

The «Toyo-Ace» SKB produced by Toyota from 1954 was the first truly successful Japanese truck. 1,500 a month were built in 1956.

The Nissan Cedric of 1960 was a typical prestige vehicle. The 15 ft (4.590 m) long body was of integral type, the engine being a 1,883 cc 4-cylinder.

The Otha PA, of which we see a model from 1953, had a 903 cc 4-cylinder engine delivering 23 hp at 4,000 rpm.

dustry was overmanned, and workers were laid off (although contrary to what is still sometimes claimed, the labor force was by no means weak in its dealings with the entrepreneurial classes). During the war labor had been organized along virtually military lines. Salaries had been far from satisfactory, and work conditions almost always oppressive. «Liberated» by the democratic principles introduced under the US occupation, most workers joined the powerful new trade unions. And when Toyota and Nissan announced massive cuts in excess labor, the response was a long series of strikes, some lasting over 100 days. It was a difficult time, and both SCAP and the Japanese government did their utmost to modify the size of the unions. Though they succeeded, the industry was left in a critical state, Nissan being saved from insolvency only by the intervention of the Bank of Japan, and Toyota hav-

The «Mikasa» company, active from 1957 to 1961, produced a series of front-wheel drive vehicles with air-cooled twin-cylinder engines delivering about 20 hp. On the left we see a convertible and a station-wagon version.

The «Aichi Machine» company founded in 1943 and absorbed into the Nissan group in 1965, built the Cony with a 354 cc horizontal twin-cylinder engine. A 1963 version is shown above.

ing to renew all its top management. Nevertheless peace was restored, and new labor-management relations were established which then became almost idyllic. In place of the national unions, more peaceable company unions were formed, and «collateral» benefit policies were introduced for employees, most importantly in the areas of social assistance and leisure. Also introduced was the «life employee» system by which workers became joined to their companies as to a second family, with pay adjusted according to seniority. A gap emerged between large and small businesses, the latter having less qualified labor, with considerably lower salaries and less attractive benefits. The working classes thus became stratified according to the size of the firm in which they worked. Selection began in childhood, a meritocratic system insuring that entrance to the best schools and universities was through tough competition. Everybody's ambition was to join the best companies and offer them the utmost loyalty and commitment. Efficiency and productivity at the same time became a means to social advancement and a better standard of living.

The third negative factor in the state of the Japanese car industry in the early fifties was the low level of technology. It was not that there were no good designers (much precious experience had been gained in the armaments sector during the war); the problem was rather that no-one had the first idea how to make a low-cost car for mass production that would be both adequate in quality and attractive to the eye. Where possible, lessons were learnt from the West, but the quickest way of closing the all too obvious technological gap was by embarking on joint-ventures with US or European manufacturers. Nissan was the first to move in this direction, agreeing to a contract with Austin in 1952 to produce A40 cars under license. The following year Mitsubishi reached a similar agreement with the Kaiser Motor Co. to assemble Jeeps in Japan, and Isuzu and the Roots group collaborated to produce a Japanese version of the Hillman Minx. Hino meanwhile started a production line for 4CV Renaults.

Gradually imports even of components lessened, and by 1958 the «nationalization» of the entire production process was complete, all the assembly plants of Japanese manufacturers being supplied with Japanese-made components. Production rose steadily, reaching 308,020 in 1960, of which 128,984 were standard range cars, and 165,094 economy cars under 360 cc.

The Japanese miracle

In the sixties a number of factors combined which were all to have a decisive effect on the spectacular growth of the Japanese car industry.

Of a total of 1.3 million vehicles on the roads of Japan in 1960, only 457,333 were cars (one per every 240 of the population). However, the postwar economic boom was stimulating private car ownership, both for limited commercial use and for family transport. Economic progress in the wake of the Korean war, together with the introduction of democratic principles under the US occupation, had already considerably altered the traditional view whe-

reby state interests took automatic precedence over private interests. The steady growth of the building industry had created strong demand for trucks, while at the same time the advantages of road transport both for supply and distribution of materials and semi-worked goods for industry were becoming increasingly apparent. Employees' improved living standards (the annual rate of salary increases was extremely high) and social position, together with greater leisure, led companies to introduce more recreation facilities: one early scheme was group holidays, which greatly stimulated internal tourism, and for which large coaches were usually required. Another result of the industrialization of the country was the growth of suburbs around the big industrial cities. Individual mobility thus became an ever more keenly felt necessity, and increasing individualism meant that no development of the public transport system, however good, could satisfy this need. Car-owner status became an ever more significant factor, even though initially the requisite outlay for the purchase of a car (close to what was needed for a house) remained too great for most people to afford; in 1965 only 5.7% of families had a car of their own. Nevertheless the motor industry continued to grow in importance in the Japanese economy, overtaking the electric and communication equipment industry in 1963. In this it was helped by a deliberate government policy of encouragement. On the international front, after the war, rigid protectionist barriers were created, based on high import levies and a quota system. For over 20 years taxes on foreign cars stood at about 35% for «large cars» and 40% for «small cars». Only in 1968 did these barriers begin to be lifted, in response above all to US pressure. A block on foreign investments in Japan also prevented the agreements with Western manufacturers (especially the «Big Three» US companies) from becoming, as they easily might have, an effective takeover of the still emergent Japanese car industry by foreign capital.

The system of taxation in the field of car manufacture and development also played an important role. Cars were classed in three groups, according to their displacement: standard (over 2,000 cc), small (between 361 and 2,000 cc), and midget (less than 360 cc). Midgets were particularly well suited both to the average Japanese family's budget and current road conditions in Japan, and sales of this category were promoted by financial incentives. The tax payable on a midget was much less than for a 1,000 cc car, the road tax being less than two thirds of that for the more powerful models, and the purchase tax being a third lower, with the added advantage of no obligatory overhaul (and hence no service charges of that kind). These tax arrangements have been retained up until the present time (in 1976 the midget class specification was raised to 550 cc), but they really only had a significant effect on sales in the early days: in the second half of the sixties the proportion of total production being roughly 25%, declining steadily to 3% in 1984. The state of the road network was another important factor affecting exports to Japan. Even in 1970 only 1% of the roads were metaled, with no more than 10% being hard enough for heavy transport; about two thirds of the overall milage of roads were unfit for motor transport. This made foreign cars, built as they

HINO

Hino, which was established in 1942, entered the automobile sector by manufacturing the Renault 4CV under license from 1953 to 1961. In the latter year they brought out their first original car, the Contessa (above), with an 893 cc 4-cylinder Renault-inspired rear engine, delivering 35 hp at 5,000 rpm. On the right is the coupé version designed by Michelotti, which came out in 1962 with the power increased to 45 hp. In 1964, the series was completely redesigned by the same Italian and given a new 1,251 cc engine capable of developing 55 hp in the sedan version and 65 hp in the coupé version (see below left and right). The company was taken over by Toyota in 1966.

were for «tamer» road conditions, virtually unusable outside the big towns, and at the same time encouraged the home industry to produce vehicles designed to cope with local conditions. A period of expansion and intense competition began for the car industry. As has already been indicated, this area of industry was (with the exception of Mitsubishi) developed outside the great *zaibatsu* empires by small, brave entrepreneurs such as Kiichiro Toyoda and Soichiro Honda, who represented an emerging class of businessmen on the edges of the so-called Japan Inc., concentration of political, financial, and industrial power interests. Car manufacturers were thus not politically significant at the highest levels, and it was not until 1972 that a member of this sector of industry was elected to

PRINCE

After having built a series of electric vehicles under the TAMA trade-name, Prince began producing its first gasoline-engined car in 1952, a 1,484 cc 4-cylinder sedan which was named «Skyline» in 1955. This model, which had a power of 73 hp at 4,800 rpm and a speed of approximately 80 mph (130 km/h), made its international debut at the Paris Motor Show in 1957. In 1961, the «Gloria» (left) appeared with an identical body and more luxurious finish, an engine displacement of 1,862 cc and power of 84 hp. In 1964, the two models were further differentiated with the introduction of the new series with de Dion rear axles. The 1.5-liter Skyline, designed by Michelotti (below right) kept the old 4-cylinder engine, while the new Gloria (below left) was given a new 1,988 cc 6-cylinder, 106 hp at 5,400 rpm (subsequently used on the Skyline as well). Above left is the Skyline Sport as drawn by Michelotti in 1963, and right the pick-up of the same year which is similar in style. In 1966, the company was taken over by Nissan who continued producing the two Prince models under its own name.

a prominent public position with the nomination of Katsuji Kawamata, managing director of Nissan and president of JAMA (Japan Automobile Manufacturers Association) as vice-president of the prestigious and powerful KEIDANREN, Japan's major business association.
As a result of all this, the car industry evolved with almost complete freedom of competition. There were two

consequences of this. On the one hand productivity steadily rose, so cars became cheaper and hence available to a wider market; for instance, the price of a 1,500 cc car dropped from $3,000 in 1955 to $1,500 in 1965, while during the same period national income per capita rose 3.5 times, from $210 to $710. «Car fever» thus became widespread, with cars sometimes coming before houses on the

A prototype of the Mazda Cosmo 110S was unveiled at the Tokyo Motor Show of 1964. Initially, the twin-rotor Wankel engine had a total displacement of about 800 cc for a power of 70 hp at 6,000 rpm.

scale of necessities, symbolizing the new standard of living. On the other hand, the number of different car producers (11 in 1960) created practical problems. In the late fifties a great deal of money was invested in new car factories, indicating that the traditional bias in favor of industrial vehicles had shifted. The years 1959 and 1960 saw the erection of impressive new factories, among which one might cite Motomachi (Toyota), Oppama (Nissan), Fujisawa (Isuzu), Murayama (Prince) and Hamura (Hino). Yet the constant rise in demand was such that the big manufacturers could still not produce enough. Thus even more investment was needed, also in the areas of distribution and servicing facilities, research and new development, as well as in improving working conditions. Investment in factories in this sector of industry alone, between 1960 and 1963, came to over 264 billion yen. However, the size of

the individual companies was considerably below that suggested by such financial commitment, and below that of Western companies. Average companies like BMC, Volkswagen, Renault and Fiat had two or three times the turnover of Toyota and Nissan, one to two times the profits, and five to eight times the number of employees. Then, despite their considerable profits, the Japanese manufacturers were having to set aside a substantial outlay on a marketing network, there being no system of financing this area. Furthermore, the high turnover per employee in the early sixties had to be seen in the light of the relatively low number of employees. In comparison with Western companies there was less need for manpower in fact, since Japanese manufacturers bought many components ready-made from a myriad of smaller supply firms. For the leading Japanese producers the value added was of the order of 15-20%, as against 25-30% in Europe. Production capacity meanwhile remained relatively low: the two largest companies, Toyota and Nissan, in 1962 produced

The Honda S800 coupé of 1966 is the final version of the little sports car developed in 1962.

This Isuzu Bellett MX 1600 by the Italian designer Ghia was seen at the Tokyo Motor Show of 1969.

Honda N360

The «midget» category of vehicles with displacements of less than 360 cc played a major role in the development of Japanese motoring in the sixties. These small vehicles enjoyed certain advantages such as the fact that they could be parked by the kerb at night in cities, whereas cars of greater capacity were prohibited from doing so.

Suzuki Fronte 360

Subaru R-2

Mazda R-360

Daihatsu 360 Sedan

Subaru 360 Custom

82,000 and 97,000 cars respectively from their own factories, which was about an eighth of Italian Fiat's output that same year. The Japanese industry was thus still potentially vulnerable, in the unlikely event of an opening of the home market to imports. Government protection of the car industry continued through indirect means: protectionism at the international level, and special concessions aimed at encouraging the purchase of new equipment to modernize the production process. The car and steel industries benefited from these financial measures, which remained and indeed were even increased at times when balance of payment difficulties might have justified the government in reducing them. Direct financial help was given to the suppliers of components, meanwhile, where there was need for capital to improve productivity and rai-

se the levels of technology. A program of reorganization of this entire sector was begun in 1959 with the Temporary Law Concerning Machinery Industry Promotion, financed through the Japan Development Bank and the Small Business Finance Corporation to the tune of about $50 million, loaned at subsidized rates. This raised productivity and tightened up the sector. In the second half of the sixties, while continuing to offer no direct support to the car industry (where laws of natural selection based on competitive strategy reigned), MITI made some proposals for «concentration,» some of which were adopted, and others of which were dropped in the face of opposition from the smaller businesses who wished to keep their own character and independence.

Seven mergers were suggested between 1966 and 1968, with

Numerous «dream cars» were introduced in the late sixties, in which careful consideration was given to safety features as well as styling. On the facing page we see the Nissan prototype of 1966 (above) and the Toyota EX-I of 1969, which inspired the Celica line of the following year. Above is the Toyota EX-III of 1969 and below, the Mazda RX-500.

only three actually occurring: Nissan taking over Prince, and Toyota taking over Hino and Daihatsu.

Throughout the decade Japanese car production rose at a tremendous rate, the 1960 total of 165,100 leaping to 407,800 in 1963, and to 696,200 in 1965. In 1966 for the first time car production exceeded that of industrial vehicles. In 1967 the million mark was crossed, with total production of 1,375,800, rising the following year to 2,055,800, making Japan the world's fourth biggest car producer, beating France and Italy. The total for 1970 was 3,178,700.

The increase in car ownership during the sixties made it possible for the industry to plough its profits back into new production technology, and this, together with excellent labor relations, soon brought productivity levels considerably above those of Western companies. As well as the factors already described, other domestic policies had contributed to this achievement, such as tax reductions on both car ownership and fuel. The overall cost of keeping a car (of equivalent engine size) was about a third less than the average in Europe. However, this changed radically in 1971 when the state undertook a five-year road building plan, thus removing one of the last barriers to car driving in Japan. At this date a «weight tax» on motor vehicles was introduced, and this now makes car ownership in Japan considerably more expensive than in the West.

The internationalization of the seventies

Parallel with the development on the home market, the Japanese car industry had also ventured into the world market, initially in the developing countries of Asia, and then in the more advanced West.

The first Japanese vehicles to be exported after the war left the country in 1947, but it was only around the mid fifties that exports really became significant in quantity. Cars were still secondary, and even in 1955 all the 1,231 vehicles dispatched from Japan were trucks and buses. Furthermore, they went to only a limited number of countries, especially Taiwan, Okinawa (at that time administered by the USA), Thailand, South Korea and Brazil. In 1956 a mere 46 cars sold to these countries, but thereafter the figures grew rapidly, reaching 7,013 in 1960 (32% of all exported vehicles). Alongside this purely commercial development, from 1959 Japanese vehicles were also sent for American military use in Southeast Asia (17,000 in 1963). Total Japanese exports in 1963 touched 100,000, including 31,500 cars, for which the market had

The first generation of Toyota Corolla, symbol of the internationalization of the Japanese automobile industry, was introduced in November 1966. Available in a two- or four-door sedan and station-wagon version, the Corolla series had a newly developed 1,077 cc 4-cylinder 60 hp engine. In September of 1969 a larger 1.2-liter engine replaced the original 1.1-liter. From 1966 to 1984 the production of Corolla reached 11 millions units, 5,4 millions of which were exported. On the right is the Takaoka assembly plant.

spread to over a hundred countries: South Africa first, then Thailand, Australia, Okinawa, the United States and India. At this early stage of the internationalization process CKD (Complete Knocked Down) units played an important role. These were car kits for assembly in local plants financed either as joint-ventures between Japanese companies and local capital sources or with all-Japanese or all-local funds, according to the possibilities afforded by local legislation in each country. The first step in this direction was the setting up of Toyota do Brasil in 1958 (with Japanese capital) for assembling off-road vehicles. Over the next few years all the leading companies followed suit, with plants predominantly in Latin America (Nissan), Eastern Asia (Toyota, Nissan, Prince, Isuzu, Hino, Daihatsu and Suzuki), Australia (Toyota, Isuzu and Mitsubishi), and South Africa (Isuzu and Hino). Hino was the first to enter Europe on this basis (Spain and Greece). At first, especially in the more sophisticated markets, efforts had to be made to alter the distinctly negative image gained by Japanese vehicles before the war. To this end Japanese companies took an active part in international racing, achieving some fine rally results in the fifties, and reaching a peak in the sixties with Honda's performance in Formula 1. Japan's image was also changing as a result both of mass-produced goods of all kinds penetrating to almost every corner of the world and of the boom in tourism, with foreigners flocking to discover a country that for centuries had been so isolated. In 1957 the first Japane-

se car (a Toyota Crown) was exported to the United States, to be well received initially, then completely disregarded. Driving conditions were quite different from conditions in Japan, where cars were designed to travel at 31-37 mph (50-60 km/h) along tortuous roads that it would be euphemistic to describe as bumpy. Japanese suspension and road-holding quality were wholly unsuited to fast driving along straight highways. The bodywork even looked smaller than it actually was. And stylistically there had not been great concern to appeal to overseas taste. The first attempt at breaking into the most glittering world market had ended in a fiasco, but at least it showed Japanese manufacturers what details had to be worked on to achieve greater success. Exports grew steadily throughout the second half of the sixties, although as a percentage of overall production they stayed considerably lower than in the West, despite a rise from 14.5 to 22.8% between 1965 and 1970 (e.g. as against France's 56.7%, Germany's 55%, Britain's 42% and Italy's 36.7%). Domestic demand thus continued to be a major factor in the expansion of the Japanese car industry. Things were to change in a matter of years. In 1971 exports of cars already totaled 1,299,351, a 44.2% increase from the previous year. It should be borne in mind that up until 1978 Japanese statistics included CKD sets, which represented less than 60% of the value of the assembled vehicle. Notwithstanding the inclusion of these sets, intended for assembly in plants generally in developing countries, there is no de-

Japanese automobiles are exported using ships owned by the manufacturers themselves. Nissan has its own port at Honmoku. On the facing page, Corolla hatchbacks waiting to be loaded on to the company's ships at Toyota's Nagoya Wharf Center.

nying that the expansion of the Japanese car industry was quite unprecedented. A number of events during the seventies could have slowed this development down, had the industry not achieved full maturity. The first of these was the 1973 oil crisis, which proved so difficult for European and American companies. Specializing in small, economy cars for which the energy crisis created a sudden demand, Japan enjoyed a stroke of good fortune. Between 1973-77 exports rose from 1,450,884 to 2,538,919, with an average growth rate of 16.5%. Production fluctuated slightly over the same years, from 4,471,000 in 1973 to 3,932,000 in 1974, then up to over 5 million in 1976. Japan had now stepped into second place in the world car production ranking after the USA, having overtaken Germany in 1971. In the export field, Japan became the

world's foremost seller, overtaking Germany here in 1974. With the energy crisis the Japanese home market ended its extraordinary process of expansion, with sales settling after the rush of the sixties to around 3 million (the lowpoint of the decade being 1976, 2.4 million), where it continues to remain fairly constantly. Exports thus became an increasingly big factor in production, rising from 34.9% in 1971 to 50.5% in 1976. The growing popularity of Japanese cars on the world market could not but cause some concern to Western manufacturers, who considered the competition unfair given the differences in labor costs and productivity — key concerns behind union action in Europe (and to some degree also in the USA) — which made competitive pricing extremely difficult. Such aggressive marketing by a country still virtually closed to im-

The millionth Toyota CKD unit bound for foreign assembly plants was dispatched from the Nagoya Wharf Center in May 1976.

ports was bound to provoke defensive measures, such as the quotas stipulated in turn by France (3% of the market), Italy (about 2,000 vehicles) and Britain (10% of the market).

In USA the first signs of a desire to restrict Japanese imports had already appeared in 1970. Known in Japan as the «Shock Nixon,» a 10% supertax was put on imports, and this combined with the revaluation of the yen by about 17% threatened seriously to weaken the Japanese car industry. Washington was in part concerned to make Japan liberalize its internal economy, and in this it had some success. In 1971 duties on imported cars were dropped to 10%, and foreign investors were once again allowed into the country. However, the immediate effects of this opening up to American capital were not extensive: Chrysler and General Motors acquired minority shareholding in Mitsubishi and Isuzu respectively. Only much later, and for quite different reasons, did Ford come into Toyo Kogyo and GM increase its involvement in Isuzu and take shares in Suzuki. In fact the Japanese market did not particularly attract American companies, being so well-established in its differences, and specializing as it did in cars so far removed from standard American models. And

even when excise duties on imported cars were finally abolished in 1978, the results were extremely modest (54,517 imports rising to 64,808 in 1979, then dropping right back). It should, however, be stressed that strict licensing requirements and high transportation costs still acted as a restraint. A JAMA study made in 1980 estimated that a US compact car selling at home for $5,000 would cost just under $14,000 in Japan.

Meanwhile Japanese manufacturers had very early on brilliantly solved the problem of long-distance transportation, using ships generally owned by the car companies concerned, who often also had their own wharves. Nevertheless, after the initial aggressive attempts to «conquer» Western markets, a steadier policy of commercial expansion was pursued. Already in the early seventies, for instance, Toyota had stopped trying to sell its Crown and Mk II models in large numbers in the United States (as these competed directly with American intermediate and compact cars), and concentrated instead on the sub-compact Corona and Corolla, in competition almost exclusively only with European models. Nissan similarly concentrated on promoting the Datsun 510 and 1200 on the US market, rather than the more luxurious and up to date 610.

The Toyota RV-2 of 1972: an interesting multipurpose vehicle.

THE NEW IMAGE

TAKURI Type 3 - 1907

The first Japanese automobile was the Takuri, designed by Komano-suke Uchiyama, a dozen of which were produced by the «Tokyo Automobile Works.» The engine was an 1,850 cc horizontally-opposed twin-cylinder, while the transmission had two gear ratios. The chassis had side and cross members of steel and there was semi-elliptic spring suspension on all four wheels. The bodywork was particularly well finished. The single acetylene headlamp was a distinctive feature.

MITSUBISHI Model A - 1917

The first major industry to become interested in the automobile sector was Mitsubishi, who started producing the Model A in 1917, about twenty of which were constructed between then and 1921. The engine was an 1,846 cc 4-cylinder capable of developing 19 hp. After this brief period of automobile production, the company concentrated entirely on industrial vehicles up to 1952.

DATSUN Roadster - 1935

The first Datsun, produced in 1932, is regarded by many as a copy of the Austin Seven. Herbert Austin himself imported one from Australia (about thirty chassis had been exported to that country in 1934, the bodywork being fitted locally) to see if there were grounds for legal action, but the evidence was regarded as insufficient. The little Japanese car differed from the British one above all in the worm-drive rear axle and semi-elliptic rear springs. The Datsun of 1935-37, shown here in the roadster version, differed from its predecessors in having a slightly longer wheelbase and displacement increased from 495 to 747 cc. Production reached 15,000 units in 1937.

MAZDA - 1940

Mazda built its first automobile in 1960, but the possibility of entering the sector had already been considered before the war, a small prototype sedan (shown here) being produced in 1940. The outbreak of war prevented the company from starting mass production and this was hampered after the end of hostilities by the general veto imposed on automobile production by the occupying American forces.

NISSAN Bluebird 310 - 1959

Nissan introduced the successful Bluebird series in 1959, with the 310. This first version had a flat chassis with a rigid rear axle. The engine was a «classic» 4-cylinder in line 1,189 cc, made entirely of cast iron, with overhead valves and a lateral camshaft. The power was 48 hp SAE at 4,800 rpm. The transmission had three gear ratios with hypoid final drive. The mechanically operated brakes were of the drum type. A station-wagon version of this car was also produced, and the little Fairlady sport was built on the same mechanical basis.

SUBARU 360 - 1958

With the commencement of production of the 360 in 1958, Subaru opened up the «midget» era. This vehicle, designed by the technical staff who had created the «Zero» fighter, had a two-speed transverse twin-cylinder rear engine capable of developing about 16 hp. It was air-cooled. Features like the transmission with three synchronized gear ratios (4-speed gears were introduced in 1969) and independent torsion bars suspension on all four wheels were quite progressive for the period. The Subaru 360, a station-wagon version of which was also built, remained in production for no less than 14 years, until 1971.

HONDA S800 - 1966

The little Honda sports car introduced in 1962 (S500) with characteristics evidently derived from the motorcycle (e.g. chain gears), had highly progressive engine features. The cylinder block and head were in fact entirely made of light alloy, with «damp» cylinder barrels. The timing was of the twin overhead camshaft type, with Vee-slanted valves, while the fuel was supplied by 4-horizontal carburetors. The particularly high rotational speed (8,500 rpm) enabled a specific power of nearly 100 hp per liter to be attained. The final version which appeared in 1966 was the S800, delivering 70 hp at 7,570 rpm, and capable of a maximum speed of 100 mph (161 km/h). It had conical hypoid final drive.

DAIHATSU Fellow - 1966

The little Daihatsu Fellow came on the market in 1966. It had a front-mounted 356 cc twin-cylinder engine with a cast iron cylinder block and light alloy cylinder head and a power of 23 hp SAE at 5,000 rpm. This unit, which was water-cooled, was fed by a Mikuni-Solex inverted carburetor (a 32 hp SAE «SS» version was introduced in 1969, with two carburetors). The rear-wheel drive Fellow had 4-speed transmission with a non-synchronized first gear. The maximum speed was about 62 mph (100 km/h). It had independent front suspension with a rigid rear axle with semi-elliptic springs and hydraulically operated drum brakes.

THE TECHNOLOGICAL
ERA

While the sixties were a period of phenomenal growth at home, and the following decade saw a remarkable advance into the international market, the eighties have seen Japan become the world's largest car manufacturing country. After production of over 6 million cars in 1979, the total for 1980 leapt to over 7 million, surpassing the output of the American car industry which had been hard hit by the crises of 1973 and 1978, and which had seen productivity fall from 9.2 million in 1977 to 6.3 million. Thus the country that had led the world in car production since the very early days of the industry finally had to cede its place at the top. The policy pursued by Japanese manufacturers while they were head of the league (by 1984 the US industry had recovered and overtaken them again) was essentially one of consolidation. The upward trend of the home market had plateaued at a substantial, yet no longer increasing, demand for replacement cars, while increased exports would certainly have provoked retaliation from abroad, where Japanese imports were seen as a threat to home production. Development had therefore to be within these boundaries, both national and international (above all in relation to the West). Over the American and European industries, the Japanese producers had the great advantage of having already gone through two vital stages of evolution by the end of the seventies. Firstly, because of its relatively recent appearance on the scene, its production process was fully up to date, and as has already been noted, the government had introduced financial incentives to insure that equipment was constantly modernized. Moreover Japanese production policies had always been tailored to the conditions of the day. One example might be the introduction of the «just in time» or «Kamban» system, whereby components made by a third party ceased to be stocked, and were supplied straight to the assembly lines according to demand. This was rendered possible above all by the «hierarchical» relationship and mutual trust between the car and component manufacturing industries. The Japan Auto Parts Association includes some 20 large businesses, closely linked to the major manufacturing companies, which in turn run 300 or so average-size firms. These themselves then use a further 5,000 small companies and individual artisans, in a pyramid structure that enables the need for flexibility at the top to be filtered down to a broad groundbase.

To get a better idea of this, it is important to remember the difference between the workers in this «support» sector (representing about 45% of the total number employed in the overall production process) and those in the large manufacturing companies: they are less well qualified,

The picture above shows one stage in the soldering process (in 1976) at Toyota's Takaoka plant, opened in 1966. Below is a «Cultus» on the fully-automated soldering line of Suzuki's Kosai plant.

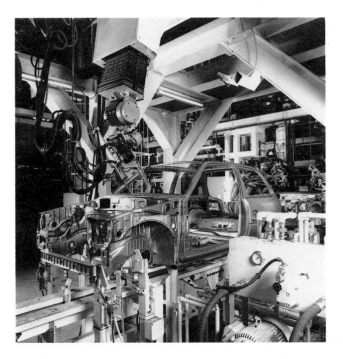

their salaries are about a third lower, and they frequently have time-contracts, all of which keeps labor costs down and guarantees flexible response to the demands of the «primary» sector. The component sector has increasingly come to supply preassembled units which enable the large companies to streamline the final assembly process even further. A feature of the Japanese car industry has been the high rise in productivity over the last 20 years or so. In the early seventies productivity was still lower than in the United States, and this was off-set only by low labor costs. Continual revaluation of the yen and the special relationship with the component manufacturing sector, as already described, enabled Japanese companies to offer salaries more attractive than in the USA. As a result, over the years Japanese productivity (in terms of production per man-hour) rose from a fifth of that in the USA in 1967, to a half in 1973, and to par in 1980. Aside from figures, the real strength of the Japanese industry lay in its highly expert management, which achieved remarkable results in optimizing the production cycle, in quality control, in the «just in time» system, and in building up efficient sales and servicing outlets. Behind these excellent results were near-ideal labor relations, with no strikes, minimal absenteeism, and an exemplary spirit of collaboration. Typical of this is the «suggestions system,» adopted especially by Nissan and Toyota, by which employees' suggestions for improving the production process or saving costs are considered, applied and rewarded. Toyota, for example, has 4,800 «Quality Circles» consisting of about ten employees each, which meet twice or three times a month to discuss and suggest to the management possible ways of improving the quality of the product. By such means, and with an already high level of automation, production rose by 151% between 1971 and 1973, with an increase in employment of barely 5.9%. Japan's streamlined production cycle gave it another edge on its American and European rivals, allowing it to offer a vast range of different models, satisfying the requirements of any «corner of the market.» In this, the development of automation played a major role, making factories much more flexible and thus lowering the financially viable minimum production levels, widening the production range of individual plants, and making them less dependent on the success of a single model (which had hitherto been so crucial). A good example is the Mazda factory at Hofu, opened in 1982, capable

A panoramic view of the Mazda plant at Hofu-Nishiura, where 20,000 finished vehicles and 7,000 CKD units are assembled each month in an area of 1,506,960 sq.ft (140,000 m²) by a staff of 1,800.

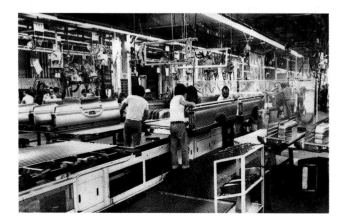

Left is the Toyota plant at Long Beach California, where assembly of the Hi-Lux pick-ups began in 1974.

of producing 27,000 cars per month (including 7,000 CKD), with a workforce of only 1,800. Here as well as the final assembly work, all the body pressing, welding and painting processes are done on lines operated by 155 robots, programmed to work on three basic models, with altogether nine different bodies. This makes it easy to tailor production to market demand, with the further advantage that the production lines can readily be adapted when models are changed. In contrast to the United States (who were surprisingly late in updating their technology and plant) and Europe (caught up in a competitive race to broaden their range of production), Japan was able to enter a new phase of development, embarking on a massive series of investments in new technology research, with an

eye to the international market first and foremost. During the years of expansion at home and abroad, Japanese competitiveness relied mainly on being able to sell cars cheaply, through strictly standardized production, despite the superior marketing and technology of their primarily European rivals. As they became more successful on the world market, they managed to adapt rapidly to offer a wider range of better quality models, though without as yet developing a distinctive style and technology, despite the introduction of certain innovations. Massive funding of research and development in the second half of the seventies, however, made possible a substantial program of change. At first this was in the form of new «gadgets» rather than in a more fundamental rethinking of car construction as such, but it then evolved into a thorough application of the most sophisticated technology, which overcame all sense of inferiority to the West. As well as the factors already noted, such as the government's financial encouragement of investment in technological research and increased productivity, there were other important factors, most notably the manufacturers' healthy financial position. Even in the years of the energy crisis, Japanese companies had maintained constant profits (Mazda alone registering a slight deficit in 1975), which had been possible to reinvest in self-supporting modernization programs. This availability of funds was and still is improved by the fact that the main shareholders are banks, who are interested less in high dividends (the dividends are thus considerably lower than in America and Europe) than in supporting company liquidity and «underwriting» quotations on the Stock Exchange. Substantial funds have thus been put into research and development, an unavoidably risky enterprise which the less financially buoyant Western companies have only been able to embark on within restrictions.

Fierce competition among local manufacturers is another ingredient in the Japanese «technological boom.» While in the USA the car industry had developed under the umbrella of the «Big Three,» which made for planned and controlled growth and in Europe it had only become more aggressively competitive after the oil crisis, in Japan the expansion process, both national and international, had always been intensely belligerent. And the battlefield then gradually changed from the marketing sphere to that of technology above all. Having first won a reputation merely for convenience, Japanese cars went on first to gain a name for reliability and quality, then to become associated with technological sophistication. Japanese producers had thus developed an export strategy in which greater profits were reaped by means of sheer superiority of quality. This made them more competitive in the industrialized world, giving them a rising trade surplus despite (especially in dealings with USA) voluntary quotas. One development now being established is the use of Japanese capital and technological support for production of cheaper, less sophisticated products in the developing countries of the East. In Korea, for instance, Hyundai (Mitsubishi) sponsored a car industry that is now venturing into Western markets with exceptionally cheap cars. Also in the eighties, Japanese companies have opened plants in Western countries, both fully independent and as joint-ventures. Among the most important of these is the Honda factory in Ohio, which produced approximately 146,000 cars in 1985, and the agreement signed with Austin-Rover for production of certain Honda models in Britain and development together of the large Legend/Rover 800 sedan. Toyota and General Motors collaborated to build a factory in Fremont (California), where the New United Motor Manufacturing company in 1984 started annual production of 240,000 Corollas (sold as Chevrolet Nova) and, as from the fall 1986, another version of the same car distributed through the Toyota sales network. Nissan meanwhile has opened a factory in Smyrna (Tennessee), while in Europe, after a none too successful agreement with Alfa Romeo for production of the Arna (based on the Japanese Pulsar), the two have collaborated on the design of a off-road model. For the US market, General Motors produces certain versions of Isuzu and Suzuki cars (in both of which companies it has financial interests). It is significant that production in the USA has, as for instance in the case with Nissan, begun with commercial vehicles and pick-ups, which were less likely to cause the United States authorities alarm since they had no effect on car market statistics. The growing competitiveness of Japanese cars internationally has always been a source of friction with Western countries, particularly the United States where, after achieving a spontaneous reduction of exports, the government has devised policies to stem Japanese expansion and bring about a real opening up of the internal market (for although all import levies have officially been abolished, other factors have continued to form effective protectionist barriers). The main achievement of the Reagan administration in the redefinition of the trading relationship between Japan and the USA has been the historic 30% revaluation of the yen agreed in September 1985 at the New York summit involving the five major industrialized nations. Japanese competitive margins suffered a severe blow, especially in the areas of low labor costs and the low purchase price of cars on Western markets. Nevertheless this served to show the Japanese industry how it could compete not merely on commercial terms through marketing strategy, but at a technological level: and this was a further stimulus to open factories in the United States and Europe. For all this, though, the home market had still once again become of prime importance, and all unnecessary expenditure was cut (more for effect than anything else, Nissan reduced the salaries of 49 top management members in 1986). From another angle, however, it is worth observing that a stronger yen meant cheaper raw materials, and this to some degree balanced out the disadvantages at the export level. Despite everything, the trade balance has remained at a comfortable $39.5 billion with respect to the US market (where Japanese cars account for about 20% of the market), and $11.1 billion with respect to the EEC — a testimony to the sound basic structure of the Japanese car industry, which has succeeded also in exporting substantially more components to the USA. As far as increased imports into Japan are concerned, apart from the factors previously mentioned, it is also up to Western manufacturers to design vehicles according to the requirements of the local market. Considering that of the 45,000 or so cars imported in 1984 (the highest import figure so far is 66,000 in 1979) the lion's share went to top range European models (Volkswagen-Audi, BMW, and Mercedes-Benz took over 76% of the total), it would seem that in fact no serious broaching of the Japanese market has really been tried, nor has a proper strategy for greater penetration of the Eastern Asian market been developed.

The evolution of design

Up until quite recently, if asked which Japanese industries were more technically advanced than Western ones, one might have listed on the fingers of one hand: photographic equipment, hi-fi, televisions, etc. In the seventies the list could have included motorcycles, and in the eighties it could most probably be headed by cars. Starting from nothing, both technically and commercially, Japanese cars have won unanimous recognition in every world market in the space of a mere three decades. Only in 1948 did SCAP permit the manufacture of low cc cars. With raw materials in short supply, the Minister for Trade and Industry decided, when allotting materials, to make the few models that Japanese producers were able to build, undergo a series of tests giving priority to those which came out best. These tests took account of weight, center of gravity, turning circle, performance in rain, braking, maximum speed and acceleration, consumption, noise, degree of dust penetration into the interior, body finish, etc., and were followed up by a 621 miles (1,000 km) run over the country's woefully inadequate roads. In some early cases windows shattered, doors stuck, and suspension systems broke beyond repair. Throughout the fifties the industry was in a formative stage, learning the basic engineering, gradually acquiring expertise in construction and design, to produce more robust cars capable of better performance. Yet it was thanks to the agreements contracted with European (especially British) manufacturers for production under license of their more advanced models that the Japanese industry really started to make headway. In fact, the cars that were made under these early contracts did not incorporate the West's most recent technology, but nevertheless they were quite appropriate for the then state of the Japanese economy and road network. Thus in 1952 Nissan began assembling Austin A40s, traditional, rugged sedans, with a 1.2-liter, 4-cylinder engine, front mounted, developing 42 hp at 4,500 rpm, and still with rigid axle rear suspension with semi-elliptic leaf-springs. Its maximum speed was 71 mph (115 km/h). By comparison, the contemporary Datsun DB4 had an 860 cc engine with side valves (20 hp at 3,600 rpm), with a maximum speed of just 45 mph (72 km/h) and general design all too reminiscent of a small truck. In 1957 Isuzu commenced production of the Hillman Minx, which was similar in design and performance to the A40, though with an older 1.3-liter engine with side valves (37.5 hp). Hino probably made a less imaginative move in entering car production with the Renault 4CV. However, this though very successful in France, was not so well suited to Japan, due largely to its rear-mounted engine (rear axle with swinging semi-axles and coil springs that were perhaps not

The technological apprenticeship of the Japanese industry was based on the production under license of European vehicles, such as the Austin A40 built by Nissan from 1952 (above left), the Hillman Minx produced by Isuzu in 1957 (left) and the Renault 4CV (above) which came out of the Hino works in 1953.

tough enough for Japanese roads). A 4-cylinder 748 cc model (21 hp at 4,000 rpm), its maximum speed was 59 mph (95 km/h). Also of no small importance was Mitsubishi's experience in assembling Jeeps, begun in 1952.

Japanese car production struck out on a slightly more original course in 1955, when Toyota, after its prewar experiments with cars based on American models (which proved unrealistic for Japan), brought out the Crown, to all intents and purposes the first modern Japanese car. Stylistically still based on American lines, mechanically it set new standards of toughness and efficiency, with a 4-cylinder engine with side valves (28 hp at 4,000 rpm). However, it was not particularly fast (max. speed 49 mph, 79 km/h), and with a deadweight of 2,755 lb (1,250 kg) it had poor acceleration. Its lack of commercial success was due largely to this poor performance (in 1957 hopes of importing to the USA were high, but the disappointment was particularly great here). The achievement of international

standards and real commercial appeal became a reality only with the launch of two historic models: the Datsun 310, or Bluebird (1959), and the Toyota Corona (1960). The former was a small sedan, obviously English in inspiration, with a 4-cylinder water-cooled engine with overhead valves and side cams (1,189 cc, 48 hp at 4,800 rpm). Typically Japanese were the 3-speed transmission, with first gear not synchronized, and the rear leafsprings rigid axle. Performance was, however, considerably better, in part because the weight had been kept down to 1,873 lb (850 kg). Despite a rather traditional chassis, the second generation Toyota Corona brought out in 1960 was considerably more successful both in production terms (almost 190,000 made in three years) and technically (thanks especially to its 4-cylinder 1,453 cc engine, introduced the following year). Japan had altogether missed out on that initial development phase which Europe and America had enjoyed between the wars, when there was a large num-

The first original, modern Japanese cars were the Toyota Crown of 1955 (left) and Datsun Bluebird of 1959 (right).

The Wankel engine used on this Mazda Familia R 100 coupé of 1969 was a twin-rotor with a displacement of 491 cc × 2 (delivering 100 hp SAE at 7,000 rpm).

ber of companies specializing in de luxe production aimed at a public both interested and knowledgeable enough to provide a stimulus for progress. In Japan the initial demand from the élite had failed to benefit the local industry, as it was satisfied exclusively by imported cars. In the West the technical experience thus gained then provided a basis for the research and development programs of the leading companies (one need only cite the Volkswagen design taken from Porsche, and the effects on standard commercial production of the thriving racing business, in which almost all the main manufacturers were involved). By contrast, in Japan research only started to receive real encouragement from public bodies and interested companies around the year 1965.

Subsequently the «Japan Automotive Research Institute» (JARI), set up with government backing, did go on to create sophisticated test and experimentation procedures. The growing demand for greater power and higher speeds led Toyota and Nissan first of all to establish advanced experimentation centers and participate ever more regularly in long distance rallies. Meanwhile the component sector also introduced its own tests for durability and quality. This expansion of research and development had by the early seventies brought the Japanese car industry to a point where it could realize its technical expertise at the commercial level, most especially on the international market. A characteristic feature of Japanese engines in particular was their high ratio of power to engine size, achieved by means of a high rate of revolutions, itself made possible by the widespread adoption of the overhead camshaft and a super-square engine design with a short stroke in relation to the bore. The small 4-cylinder 791 cc Honda engine was a good example of these improvements, achieving close to 100 hp/liter. Honda also showed considerable originality and engineering ability in its front-wheel drive 1300 sedan, with all-aluminum engine, air-cooled by means of a dual system of ducts, with air forced through cast ducts situated between the monobloc and the heads, and external fins. It was also one of the very few mass produced cars in the world to feature dry sump lubrication. The transmission and differential were built in a single unit with the engine. Another unusual feature was the twin radiator (one main, and a smaller auxiliary one) on the Subaru FF1. The auxiliary had a small, silent electrically operated fan that started to turn when the main radiator reached a certain temperature. Mazda then went its own way and began using Wankel engines in the sixties (as it still does today). Acquiring the license from NSU in 1961, it brought out its first rotary model in 1967 and continued with the rotary design stubbornly, despite the gradual disenchantment with it experienced by the other companies that had tried it (NSU, Mercedes, Citroën and General Motors). Meanwhile to catch up with standard international requirements, Japanese manufacturers had to introduce fully synchronized transmission. At the same time, during the sixties, they were already starting to popularize automatic transmission, with torque converter, even on small cc cars. The first automatic gear system produced in Japan was the two-speed «Toyoglide,» which Toyota fitted on the «Master Line» commercial station-wagon in 1959, and on the Crown the following year. Also in 1960 Mazda introduced its semi-automatic «Torque Drive» on the little R-360 coupé. While Toyota went on to provide optional automatic transmission for the Corolla and Century too, Nissan and Honda brought out 3-speed automatic versions of the Sunny and N360 (the first «midget» cars to incorporate this feature) in 1967 and 1968 respectively. Then in 1970 on the Corona Toyota introduced an automatic hydraulic torque converter operating by means of an electronic circuit. By the early seventies almost all cars had abandoned the old-fashioned chassis in favor of integral chassis with a front auxiliary frame for the engine and suspension. One exception was the Toyota Crown, with a perimeter box-type, clearly American-inspired. The normal suspension was independent, front coil springs and rigid rear axle with semi-elliptic leafsprings but this gradually changed to independent suspension on all four wheels (featured for the first time on the small Subaru 360). Some models remained atypical, however, such as the already mentioned Honda 1300 which, after a long tradition of de Dion axles on Prince cars, adopted a «cross-beam» rear axle. Although this was indeed a rigid axle with semi-elliptic leafsprings, each wheel was also linked to a long torsion bar mounted onto the opposite side of the car: an unusual design making for minimal camber and reducing the self-steering effects. Another innovation in the area of suspension was the rubber spring system mounted on the Toyota Century. As Japanese cars evolved mechanically over these years, so they did esthetically, as they pushed into the international market.

Immediately after the war, technical improvement had been accompanied by a decline in body design standards, although before the war, aside from American-inspired designs, some attractive and original bodies had been produced in Japan, notably by Nissan and Otha. The need to close the vast technological gap with the West had focused all attention onto the engineering side, and the country found itself without any bodywork designing specialist.

The Toyota Master Line, a commercial vehicle equipped in 1959 with Japan's first domestically produced automatic transmission, the Toyoglide.

Some improvement occurred with the production of European cars under license in the fifties (although the models concerned were hardly the old continent's most beautiful products), but not until 1959 did any real progress appear, when Prince sent its chief engineer to learn the

THE ITALIAN DESIGN

In the sixties, the Japanese industry often used Italian designers, three of whose creations are shown here: above, the Isuzu 117 coupé by Ghia (1966) and below, the Mazda Luce designed by Bertone (1966) and Daihatsu sport cabriolet presented by Vignale at the Turin Motor Show of 1964.

EXPERIMENTAL SAFETY VEHICLES

The technical development of the Japanese automobile in the seventies was significantly influenced by research into passive safety and the reduction of harmful fumes. Above, we see one stage of the experiments conducted by Toyota on the air bag. Left, the ESV introduced by the same company in 1972. Below, a panoramic view of the Toyota Center at Higashi-Fuji, where detailed testing of exhaust gases is carried out.

The Datsun Fairlady 240 Z which came out in 1969 was designed by Goertz, who also created the BMW 507.

basics of car design in Italy. His teacher was Giovanni Michelotti, who was commissioned to design the coupé and sports versions of the Skyline. The teaching was also to include study of prototypes and wooden models. Yet it was not easy for Prince to produce Italian-designed cars, which had been conceived with a quite different production system in mind. Sheet metal working in Japan, for instance, was completely different; and a whole range of components, nonexistent at home, had to be purchased from Italy. Prince therefore invited Italian designers over to Japan to work on the new Skyline 1900 Sport in a specially reserved part of its factory, with three hawk-eyed Japanese engineers looking on to learn the «mysteries» of the trade. However, the new model was a commercial failure, though it did act as a spur to other companies to try similar ventures. There thus appeared the Hino Contessa (sedan, coupé, and sports versions, designed by Michelotti), the Mazda Luce (by Nuccio Bertone), which even competitors agreed was an exceptionally beautiful car, and the Nissan Bluebird (by Pininfarina). Daihatsu called in Vignale to help design the «1000,» and the Isuzu 117 coupé was designed by Ghia. An exception was the Datsun 240Z, the work of the German designer Goertz, who was responsible for the BMW 507 range. Toyota meanwhile went its own way in the design field, and Mitsubishi had the Debonair styled by General Motors' head designer, Hans S. Bretzner. As the engine size of the upper range models grew, Japanese manufacturers turned increasingly to American stylistic models (due also to the greater commercial interest in the American market). One example of this was the Toyota Crown, which successfully reconciled American design standards (which in the sixties also had a considerable influence on European designs) and Japanese taste. The result of this apprenticeship was the evolution of a Japanese design style combining both Italian and American features, and this was the distinctive look of Japanese cars in the seventies. Japanese body designs had to keep strictly within the size limits set by MITI for the three categories (standard, small, and midget) of car. In the midget class especially, with a length allowance of only 10.4 ft (3.2 m), curious stylistic compromises often had to be made in order to provide enough seating room. Equally, however, it did occasionally stimulate excellent creative thinking, with a striking harmonization of function and appearance. The Honda Z (1970) is an important instance of this. For all the technological

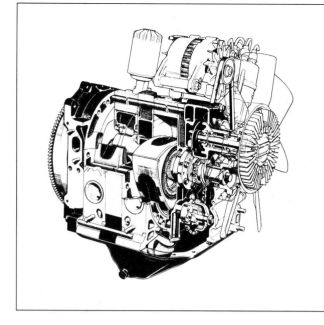

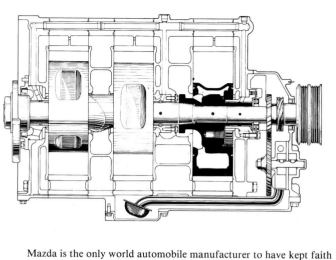

Mazda is the only world automobile manufacturer to have kept faith in the Wankel engine. On the left is the 573×2 cc 12 twin-rotor; above, the 654×2 cc triple-rotor introduced in 1985.

and design efforts of Japanese manufacturers in these early days of their expansion into foreign markets, though, the car that came to symbolize Japanese production both at home and overseas was the Toyota Corolla, which came out in 1966, and which in a sense represents all that was most traditional and «ordinary» about the industry at that time. Its sales record of about 800,000 in three years on the market demonstrates how simplicity, reliability, and toughness were sought for rather than sophisticated technology.

Three major considerations dictated the progress of the car industry in the seventies: safety, pollution, and fuel consumption. The need for improvement in each of these areas led the car industry worldwide to review its technology and bring the design and production stages closer together. Japan undoubtedly had an advantage here, in that its cars tended to be small with low cc engines, yet even so the new needs brought about some extremely interesting developments. Formerly production strategy had been to introduce new models all the time, but this now changed to technical improvement for current production, especially in the period leading up to the enforcement (in 1975) of strict antipollution legislation in Japan. The Japanese industry's ability to adapt quickly to new conditions was then given yet another opportunity to prove itself. Back in 1971 Honda had already brought out its stratified charge «CVCC» engine, while Mazda eventually succeeded in adapting the Wankel engine to comply with both home anti-pollution requirements and fuel consumption regulations in the USA. After six years' research the thirsty rotary engine's gasoline consumption had been cut by 40%. Even the small midgets were modified, their engines (usually 2- or 3-cylinder) being improved to meet market demands for greater comfort and better performance, and more and more «extras» such as automatic transmission and air-conditioning being introduced even at this bottom end of the market. First introduced by Daihatsu on its 3-cylinder Charade, and then adopted on Mitsubishi's

4-cylinder models, engines were developed with counter-rotating arms to reduce vibration. Original developments in transmission systems had also occurred, such as the Hondamatic, with hidraulic torque converter and a series of constantly engaged gears, giving exceptionally comfortable and high-performance manual selection. Mitsubishi also fitted its front-wheel drive Colt with a high-low transfer box lever, offering a range of «economy» or «power» gears. In the decade of the great energy crisis Japanese manufacturers prudently only introduced technology that had already been developed in the West, most notably transverse-engine front-wheel drive. Having once adopted that technology, however, they then explored and exploited its potential to the full. The Datsun Cherry, brought out in 1970, for example, featured that particular engine format, but with a highly individual design: the transmission underneath the engine and the differential exactly in the center, allowing for two axle shafts of identical length. Throughout the decade, however, the biggest problem facing Japanese car manufacturers were the strict anti-pollution laws introduced in Japan in 1975 and further tightened in 1976 and 1978, with maximum permissible levels of carbon monoxide (CO), unburnt hydrocarbons (HC) and nitrogen oxide (NO) fumes. The United States only introduced similarly tough measures in 1983. Catalytic silencers started to be fitted to large cc cars at the top end of the market, the more sophisticated of which already had electronic injection. «Lambda probe» systems then represented a further improvement. On smaller models compliance with regulations was attempted by means of optimizing combustion and recycling exhaust gases. Examples worth quoting might be the Honda CVCC system (mentioned above), the Mitsubishi MCA-Jet, and the Nissan NAPS-Z (Nissan Anti-Pollution System Z), all of which ran on an exceptionally lean mixture. Finally, the seventies also saw the first Japanese diesel engine (1977, powering the Nissan Cedric 220C) and the first significant use of electronics. Anti-skid braking sy-

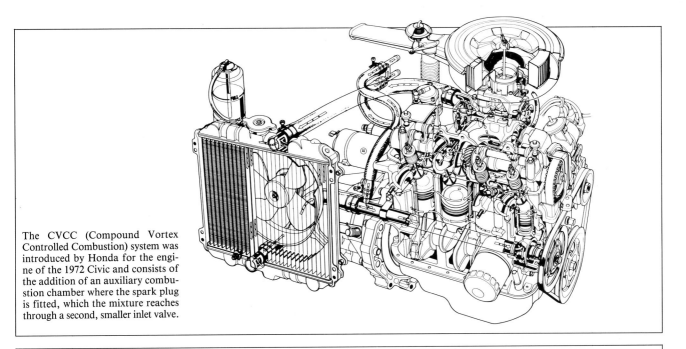

The CVCC (Compound Vortex Controlled Combustion) system was introduced by Honda for the engine of the 1972 Civic and consists of the addition of an auxiliary combustion chamber where the spark plug is fitted, which the mixture reaches through a second, smaller inlet valve.

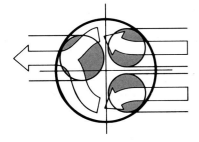

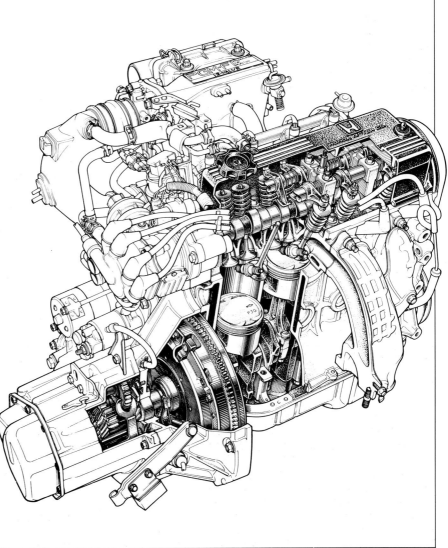

The typical timing system with 3 valves per cylinder of Honda engines of the eighties, is also used for the 1,955 cc 4-cylinder of the carburetor and fuel injection variants of the Accord/Prelude series.

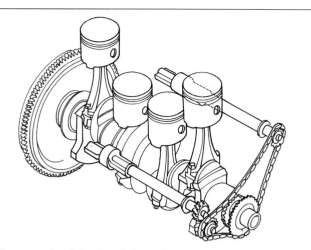

Contrarotating balancing shafts as introduced by Mitsubishi in the «Astron 80» 4-cylinder engine of 1975, can reduce the vibrations and noise typical of this type of fractionation.

stems (ECS) were developed as early as 1971, being incorporated in standard production for the first time on the Toyota Crown. The first electronic system to be fitted in a car, however, was a cruise control device fitted on the prestigious Toyota Century in 1968. Automatic transmission, fuel injection, check-control, carburetor and trip computer systems all later benefited from the new technology, making for ever greater use of electronics, with the added spur of needing to reduce fuel consumption in compliance with the new CAFE (Corporate Average Fuel Economy) regulations on the American market. Japanese manufacturers brought out experimental prototypes with so many innovations at each international car show throughout the decade that the West began to realize that it was no longer setting the pace in automobile development. In the sphere of safety, Japan also proved itself a leader, with the ESV (Experimental Safety Vehicle) presented by the Japanese industry demonstrating a practical realism that similar European prototypes perhaps lacked, being altogether too «panzer»-like for normal driving. Among the more interesting safety devices were the «drunk detector» fitted in the 1975 Nissan ESV «GR-1,» which made it impossible for an intoxicated driver to start the engine, and the rear headrest in the same model, which locked into position as soon as passengers took their seat. Stylistically, the seventies saw a return to European models, though now with a distinctively Japanese design tone, despite the still frequent use of foreign (especially Italian) designers. Mitsubishi, for instance, employed the freelance Aldo Sessano for the successful Lancer (1980), while other companies began to conceal the fact that foreign designers were working for them. In the mid seventies there first emerged the concept of the space-wagon, which was to become so popular in the next decade.

The fifth generation Corolla/Sprinter came out in 1983, with a range of 4-cylinder engines: 1,295, 1,452 and 1,587 cc (gasoline) and 1,832 cc (diesel). Here illustrated the 4-door notchback sedan Corolla (below) and Sprinter (right).

Above, the Nissan VG30 E 6-cylinder Vee block engine of 1985, with a displacement of 2,960 cc and power of 160 hp at 5,600 rpm. On the right is the Toyota «3 S» experimental engine of the same year, a turbocharged 1,998 cc 4-cylinder with intercooler and four valves per cylinder.

One of the earliest versions of this was the Toyota «MP-1» prototype presented at Tokyo in 1975, an original and versatile station-wagon, higher than normal, and featuring sliding side-doors at the rear. Japanese cars could now be said to have matured fully, having shed all sense of technical inferiority with regard to the West. In the eighties development of new technology and improvement of already existing models enabled the Japanese car industry to replace its now inappropriate commercial aggressiveness with a new kind of «aggressiveness» based on sheer quality. Undaunted by European and American rejection of certain innovations, it embarked on a thorough reexamination of the function of cars. Japan is no longer associated with production of small, cheap vehicles. While in 1974 cars over 2000 cc represented only 2.8% of overall production, rising to 6.8% in 1984, the percentage of midgets dropped sizeably between 1970 and 1980, from 23.6% to no more than 2.8%. Once the problems raised by pollution and consumption factors had been overcome, Japanese manufacturers entered a period of unhindered development of car technology. Market demands were for ever more powerful, comfortable, and reliable cars, and virtually every element of car construction underwent some change, incorporating either electronics or new materials. Thus in 1980 22.3% of cars sold in Japan had electronic injection, while by 1984 the percentage had risen to 33.7%. The search for ever better performance has resulted in per-

Nissan developed a variable nozzle ceramic turbocharger in 1985, which was used on the VG30 PROTO engine of the CUE-X concept car. The turbocharger incorporates a variable nozzle on the turbine inlet, comprising an electronically controlled flap that is adjusted in accordance with the exhaust gas flow to alter the cross sectional area of the nozzle throat and hence the ratio of that area to its radial distance from the center of the turbine.

Toyota AXV

Toyota EX-8

Mazda MX-02

Toyota Windy Cruiser

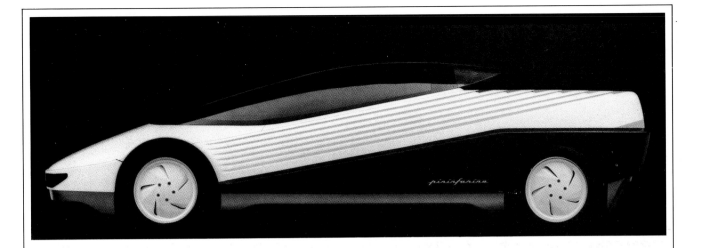

The prototype Honda HP-X (above and right) unveiled at the Turin Motor Show in 1984 was produced by Pininfarina using light composite materials such as Kevlar and carbon fibers. The engine is a 1,996 cc 6-cylinder Vee; cylinder block derived from those used in Formula Two vehicles. Below, the prototype designed by Michelotti in 1986, based on the central-engined Toyota MR-2.

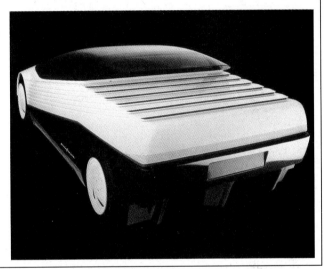

The prototype of the Nissan NX-21 of 1985.

The Nissan NX-21 prototype is driven by a ceramic gas turbine, the most promising alternative to the traditional engine. Of the twin-shaft type with a heat exchanger, it is capable of delivering 100 hp. The maximum temperature of the crown is 1,350°C. The speed of rotation of the compressor rotor is 100,000 rpm; that of the main rotor, 75,000 rpm.

fection of turbocharger supercharging systems, with the introduction first of water-cooled turbines (those made by IHI are used by Ferrari and Maserati), then of those with variable stroke (developed by Nissan for the 1985 versions of its own Cedric and Gloria models). Four valves per cylinder is now a not uncommon feature of Japanese cars, which have also made great strides in the field of «lean

One of the most sophisticated Japanese-made dashboards is that of the Nissan Soarer introduced in 1986.

burn» engines running on a very lean mixture, and thus making for greater fuel-efficiency. Continuous improvement of fuel injection systems, and introduction of new materials (such as ceramics capable of withstanding the higher combustion temperatures of such engines), have contributed vitally to this process. One of the most important steps towards an engine with reduced heat exchange, wherein many believe the future of car technology to lie, was the «Ceramik Aska» brought out by Isuzu in 1985. This had no cooling system. Turbocompressors and ceramic swirl chambers type for diesel engines are now a reality in the Japanese car industry, which in the first half of the eighties also took to using compound materials. Honda for instance has produced a steel connecting rod bound in cast aluminum. Electronics, having been used to perfect engine and automatic transmission systems, is now entering the realm of chassis construction. «CCV» (Control Configured Vehicle) technology for regulating the steering, suspension and braking properties of cars has led to a sudden revision of standards of road-holding, positive safety, and comfort. The steering wheel is becoming a transmitter of impulses sending the driver's instructions to an artificial «intelligence»; suspension is now designed to maintain optimum ground-to-tire contact, rather than merely passively cushion the vehicle over rough surfaces; brakes are now capable of stopping a vehicle on any surface without skidding and within the shortest space that is physically possible. To give some examples, the Nissan Bluebird Maxima (1984) features a 3-position electronic system for automatically adjusting the rigidity of the suspension (independently front and rear), operated by an ultrasonic «sonar» that measures the height of the car's nose from the ground, relaying the frequency of movement onto the horizontal plane, in combination with a se-

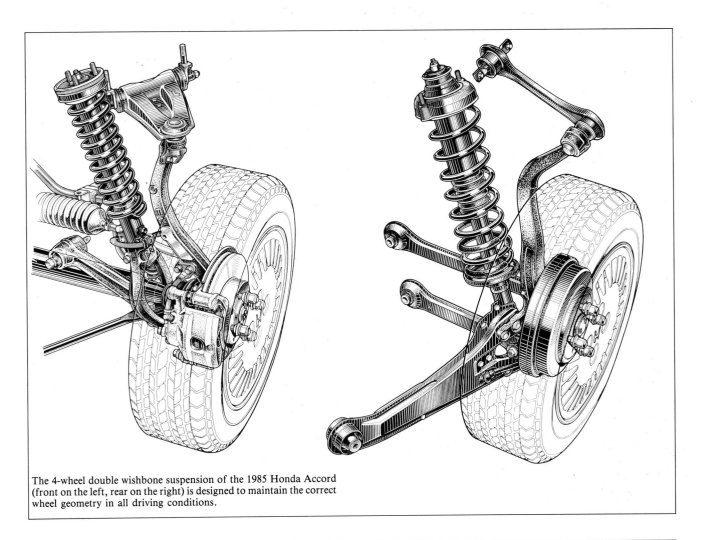

The 4-wheel double wishbone suspension of the 1985 Honda Accord (front on the left, rear on the right) is designed to maintain the correct wheel geometry in all driving conditions.

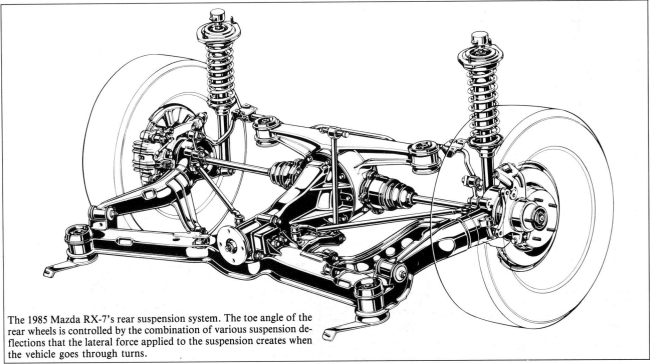

The 1985 Mazda RX-7's rear suspension system. The toe angle of the rear wheels is controlled by the combination of various suspension deflections that the lateral force applied to the suspension creates when the vehicle goes through turns.

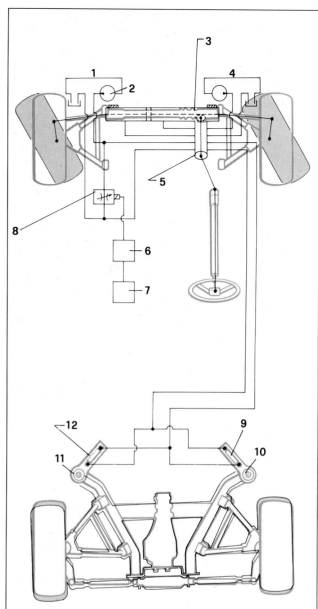

ries of sensors taking account of factors such as speed, steering angle, engine load, gearbox clutch and brakes. In 1983 Nissan also introduced servo-steering (EPS: Electronic Power Steering), hydraulically operated, giving progressive assistance according to data supplied by a small computer and the level of assistance chosen (out of three possible settings) by the driver. Finally, Mazda, Nissan, and Toyota have all produced prototypes with four-wheel steering (FWS) system, which steers the front and rear wheels in opposite directions to describe a lock to lock at low speeds, or steers them in parallel at high speeds (usually above 25 mph, 40 km/h), for superior stability on cornering. This is a very recent innovation, though like all experimental prototypes brought out by Japanese companies it has been fully tested, and now only remains to be integrated into regular production by the marketing divisions. Electronically controlled four-wheel drive systems are at a similar stage. New technology has also increased the comfort and safety of both driver and passengers. For a long time, electronics in the car world meant (quite mistakenly) mere gadgetry. Sophisticated gadgets are in fact just a visible indication of the high degree of perfection reached by much more basic and useful electronic technology. LED or liquid crystal display panels, which are now standard on many models, thus go together with safety devices such as the «sleep detector» introduced on the Nissan Bluebird in 1983. Then of course there are also electronic direction systems, operating on the principle of the compass, with memorized maps and electronic compass.

1-HICAS hydraulic circuit; 2-HICAS hydraulic pump; 3-steering gear; 4-power steering hydraulic circuit; 5-hydraulic pressure control valve; 6-controller; 7-vehicle speed sensor; 8-electromagnetic valve; 9-power cylinder; 10-suspension member insulator; 11-suspension member insulator; 12-power cylinder.

One of the four-wheel drive systems introduced by Japanese companies is shown in this diagram of the «HICAS» developed by Nissan for the CUE-X, accompanied by an hydraulic system which allows the rear wheels to be steered in the opposite direction from the front ones at low speeds, thereby improving maneuverability (above).

1-air spring; 2-strut; 3-lateral links; 4-power cylinders for maneuverability steering; 5-strut; 6-diagonal A-arm; 7-anti-roll bar; 8-HICAS power cylinders; 9-rear suspension member.

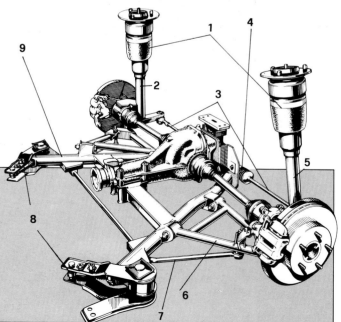

The EV-20 prototype electric car unveiled by Toyota in 1985 uses the vector control type AC induction motor. This system uses the latest power transistor and control technology to develop high efficiency and response equal to that of the DC motor system as well as to achieve low noise levels. Maximum output: 25 kW at 10,000 rpm; maximum speed 62 mph (100 km/h); maximum distance on one charge at 25 mph (40 km/h) 75 miles (120 km).

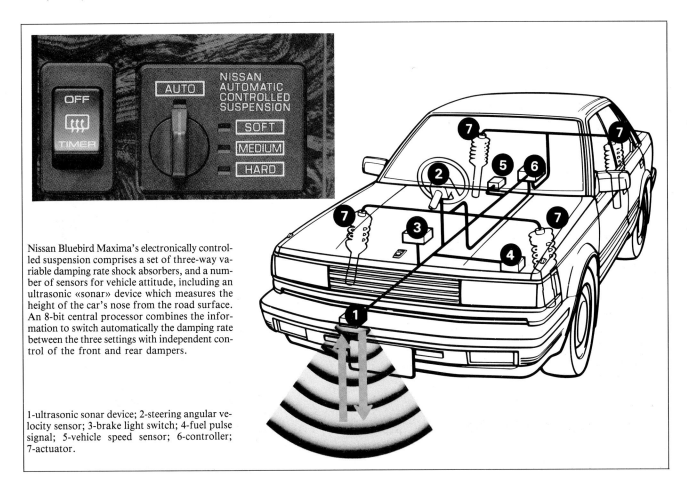

Nissan Bluebird Maxima's electronically controlled suspension comprises a set of three-way variable damping rate shock absorbers, and a number of sensors for vehicle attitude, including an ultrasonic «sonar» device which measures the height of the car's nose from the road surface. An 8-bit central processor combines the information to switch automatically the damping rate between the three settings with independent control of the front and rear dampers.

1-ultrasonic sonar device; 2-steering angular velocity sensor; 3-brake light switch; 4-fuel pulse signal; 5-vehicle speed sensor; 6-controller; 7-actuator.

KOREA: A NEW «PIVOT» IN THE CAR INDUSTRY

The birth of South Korea in the automobile industry is represented by the entry of the industrial giant Hyundai in 1967. Using initially the technology supplied by the British Ford, Hyundai began in 1968 the production of the «Cortina», to be then followed one year later by the construction of industrial vehicles. In 1972 an agreement was signed with Daimler Benz giving them license for the production of buses. In 1976 Pony's station-wagon and pick-up versions were launched. Three years later Hyundai began to export its cars however it wasn't until 1982 with the new Pony version that the export volume increased. The following year (in which the 500,000th Pony was produced) the «Stellar,» a 1.4- and 1.6-liter sedan, was introduced to the market. That same year Hyundai took its first step towards internationalization by opening a branch in Canada. In 1985 Hyundai began its production of the new «Excel» available in both hatchback and notchback versions. The «Excel,» it too supplied with technology by Mitsubishi (who owns 15% of the Hyundai capital stock), was exported in large numbers mainly to the USA and Canada. Due to the local low cost of labor new enterprises were begun in Korea. Consequently the Ford/Mazda joint-venture gave birth to KIA, which assembles cars of the Nippon company since 1977. Meanwhile General Motors, with Nissan technology developed a production line through DAEWOO. Altogether in 1986 the Korean production of passenger cars has reached the 350,000 mark.

The Hyundai Pony Excel of 1985 in the hatchback version (above). The Stellar sedan of 1983 and the 1982 version of the Pony. On some markets, these are known as the Sterling and Imperial, respectively.

A few European cars have made use of Japanese technology in the eighties, according to a series of agreements with the constructors. On the facing page, above, the Triumph Acclaim and center, the Rover 213, based on the 1979 and 1983 versions of the Honda Civic notchback, respectively. Below, the Ford Laser based on the Mazda 323 and produced in Australia, and the Arna, an automobile manufactured by Alfa Romeo with a Nissan Pulsar body and Alfasud engine. Right, the Italian Innocenti 990 with a Daihatsu 3-cylinder engine; below, the only European car manufactured under license in Japan: the Volkswagen Santana, produced in Nissan plants.

Little extras include devices like the sonar that emits increasingly louder signals when the car is reversing closer towards an obstacle (the Nissan Cedric and Laurel were equipped with this in 1983), or automatically operated windscreen wipers that respond to «rain sensors» on the hood which, being sensitive also to the pressure of rainfall, even regulate the speed at which they clear the windscreen. Alongside such innovative features, Japanese cars in the eighties have also continued to develop in terms of traditional mechanical and styling design. For example, in 1980 only 21% of the cars sold in Japan were frontwheel drive, while by 1985 this figure had risen to around 70%. During the same period the number of cars with twin overhead camshaft distribution rose from a negligible 0.3% to 9% (approximately), and turbo models have increased from 0.2% to 10%. Having learnt the basic technology from the West in the sixties, therefore, Japanese car manufacturers in the next decade went on to prove their competitiveness in terms of creativity and productivity on the international market. Eventually, through a combination of sophisticated technology and advanced marketing techniques, and generally full-blooded industrial strategy, Japanese cars gained a leading position in the world arena. Undoubtedly conditions at home, both political and social, were extremely favorable during these 30 years, but the results achieved in production abroad (especially in the USA) in the eighties can only be seen as a further testimony to attitudes and organizational abilities that are universally valid.

By the year 1990 a third of all the passenger cars produced in Henry Ford's native land will be Japanese, at least in design.

FROM COPY
TO INNOVATION

Toyota Corolla-1970

Mazda Grand Familia 808-1971

Mazda Savanna RX-7-1978

Toyota Celica-1970

Nissan Gazelle-1979

Nissan Gloria-1979

Mitsubishi Lancer Celeste-1975

74

Mitsubishi Galant coupé-1976

Toyota Crown-1971

Datsun 510-1977

Top, Mitsubishi Colt-1977

Datsun 810-1976

Datsun Cherry-1978

Subaru Leone station-wagon 4WD-1979

Mazda 323-1977

Nissan Patrol-1980

Isuzu Trooper-1981

Suzuki SJ 413-1984

Nissan Junior-1970

Above left, Mazda B-Series pick-up-1985

Left, Subaru 4WD pick-up-1979

Bottom, Mitsubishi L 200 Longbody-1985

Toyota Hi-Lux pick-up-1972

Honda Civic hatchback-1985

Honda Civic 4WD wagon-1985

Honda Civic CRX-1985

Honda Civic 4-door sedan-1985

Mazda MX-81-1982

Opposite above, Toyota Celica GT-Four-1985

Nissan NX-21-1985

Right, Toyota FXV-1985

Toyota MR-2-1984

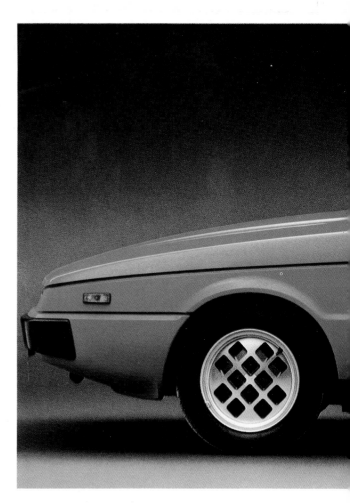

Mitsubishi Cordia-1981

Isuzu Piazza-1981

Nissan Silvia-1983

Mitsubishi Starion-1982

Mazda 727C-1984

Williams-Honda FW-09-1984

Toyota Celica Twin Cam Turbo-1985

Mitsubishi Pajero-1985

NISSAN 300 ZX-1983

The 300 ZX derived from
the successful Fairlady Z
series (inaugurated in 1969)
was produced in 1983 in
two bodywork variants,
with 2 and 2 + 2 seats. This
car has a 2,960 cc V6 engine with electronic fuel injection in the aspirated 160
hp (SAE Net) at 5,200 rpm
and turbocharged 200 hp
(SAE Net) at 5,200 rpm
versions. It has 5-speed
transmission. In the racing
sector, the 300 ZX is successfully employed in the
IMSA series by the Bob
Sharp Racing team.

Mazda RX-7-1985

Mazda MX-03-1985

Suzuki R/S1-1985

NISSAN CUE-X

The CUE-X's VG30 Proto is one of the most advanced example of reciprocating engine art. Setting targets of more than 300 hp, the engineers took three fundamental approaches: increased volumetric efficiency, enhanced induction and reduced energy losses. The 2,960 cc 24 valves V6 engine is equipped with one (variable nozzle type) turbocharger with a ceramic turbine for each bank of the cylinder «Vee». An intercooler cools the turbocharged intake air by means of refrigerant circulation. Injection, ignition (coils are mounted directly above each spark plug) variable impedance aspiration, latent heat type cooling, valve timing and throttle are electronically controlled. Power is delivered to all four wheels via an «intelligent» full-time FWD-System incorporating an electronically controlled continously variable torque split that ensures optimum traction on every road surfaces.

Supporting CUE-X is an electronically controlled air suspension system at all four-wheel, giving automatically variable spring and damping rates. CUE-X's 4-wheel-steering-system (HICAS) controls the steering angle of the rear wheels within the range permitted by distortion of the suspension bushes for improved high-speed stability.

BE-1

This 1985 Be-1 prototype small city car developed by Nissan according to the latest technology has carefully-developed aerodynamic features.

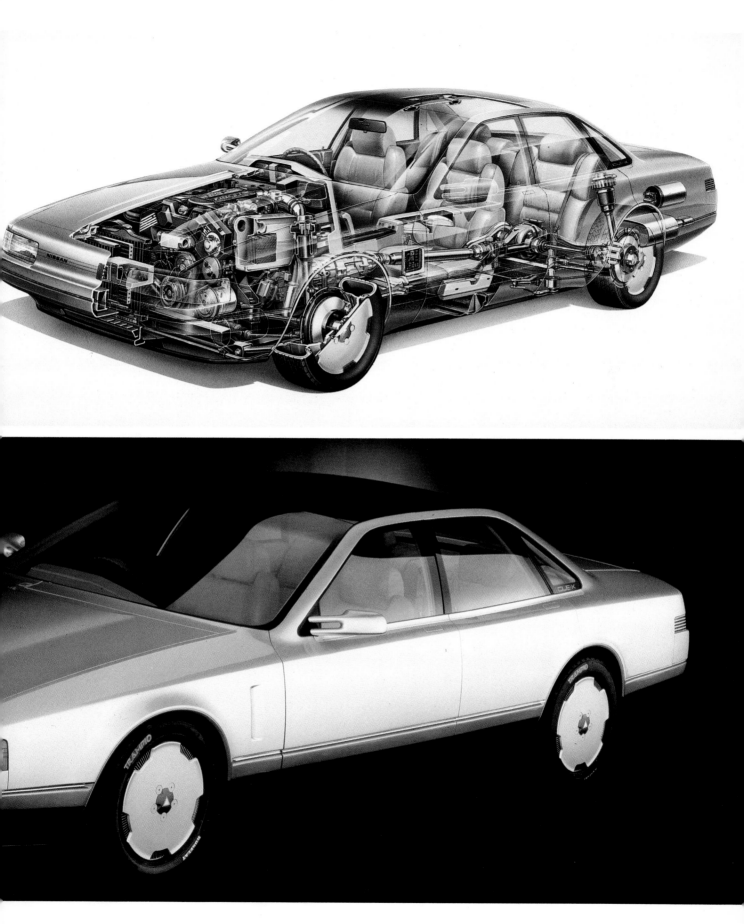

Honda Accord 4-door sedan-1985

Honda Accord LXi hatchback-1985

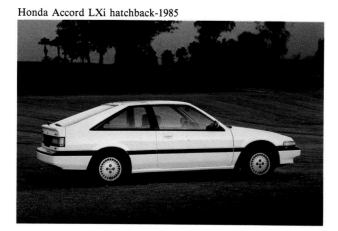

Honda Prelude 1.8-1985

Mitsubishi Galant Sigma-1985

Nissan Soarer 3.0 GT-1986

Nissan Sentra-1986

Toyota Supra-1985

Nissan MID 4-1985

JAPAN
IN INTERNATIONAL
MOTOR RACING

The Japanese Grand Prix

The development of the automobile industry in Japan was not accompanied by the growth of small engineering firms of the type associated in the West with the first heroic sporting enterprises and memorable battles on the big international circuits. The history of motor racing in Europe would probably have been far less inspiring if it had been written by the industrial giants alone. It is doubtful whether the French motor racing tradition would have been the same without the contribution of companies such as Bugatti or Delage and of course, the racing sector was responsible for the commercial growth of small stables like Ferrari and Lotus. In Japan, on the other hand, 30 years of frenetic expansion on the international markets left the companies with little room for major sporting programs, with the single exception of Honda, who on two occasions intrusted the image of its industrial and technical progress to Formula One racing vehicles. The Japanese automobile industry only started up before World War Two and was still in its infancy in the immediate postwar period, with too much to learn to think about taking on adversaries like Mercedes or Alfa Romeo, but the archipelago soon caught the racing fever. Pioneers such as Komanosuke Uchiyama had in fact been involved in the design of rudimentary racing vehicles at the beginning of the century, while in the thirties, small single-seaters like the Datsun 747 cc, mechanically derived from that company's first vehicles, were fighting it out on the Tawagawa circuit, at the very time the 520 hp of the 16-cylinder central engine were carrying the Auto Union Type C designed by Ferdinand Porsche to victory over 6,214 miles (10,000 km) away. But not until the sixties were Japanese and European vehicles to compete directly against one another in that first Japanese Grand Prix of 1963, which signaled the entry of Japan into the field of modern motor racing. The local vehicles lined up on the Suzuka circuit that May 4, were not true racers, just souped-up versions of cars like the Nissan Fairlady 1500 and Prince Skyline, while the batch of European competitors sent by the organizers was impressive, with a few Ferrari 250 LM, Lotus 23, Porsche Carrera 2 and Aston Martin DB4's. The winner was a Lotus, but a Fairlady won the Touring class: a minor achievement, but one which augured well for the future. Already by the second edition of the Grand Prix in 1964, the Japanese were entering better prepared vehicles in the Touring class, such as the Prince Skyline 2000 GT, Nissan Bluebird SS 1200 and Isuzu Bellett GT, while Honda, who had instituted their Formula One program, entered the S600 GT. Absolute victory went to a Porsche 904. There was no Grand Prix in 1965 and this interval gave

the Japanese companies time to develop their first genuine Sports Prototypes. The first in the series was the Prince R380 built in conformity with Group 6 international regulations. The central engine was a 1,996 cc twin overhead camshaft 6-cylinder, capable of delivering 200 hp, mounted on a chassis derived from that of the Brabham-Repco BT8. The new prototype had a top speed of 174 mph (280 km/h). New, more competitive Grand Touring cars were introduced by Toyota that year, with the 2000 GT and by Nissan with the Fairlady GT, while Hino prepared a 1.3- liter Contessa, Group 6 prototype with a central engine. In May 1966, when the third Japanese Grand Prix opened to inaugurate the new Fuji circuit, the national industry thus looked much more competitive. The Prince 380's managed to beat the Porsche 906's, dominating the race and finishing first and second. Daihatsu had also prepared a prototype called P3, with a 1,261 cc 4-cylinder front-engine, delivering 110 hp. The following year, not even the new Nissan R380-AII's, derived from the earlier Prince prototypes (this company had recently been taken over) could compete with the Porsche 906's. A few Group 71 prototypes also appeared in 1968, corresponding to those used in the Can-Am series, such as the Toyota 7, equipped with a 2,981 cc V8 engine with a Nippondenso injection system. Its chief rival was the Nissan R381, equipped with a Chevrolet 5,461 cc engine delivering 450 hp and characterized by a rear stabiliser clearly inspired by that of the Chaparral 2F, the incidence of which could be varied by means of a hydraulic circuit connected to the rear suspension. This won the race. The 1969 edition of the Japanese Grand Prix (open to Groups 4, 6 and 7) assumed world status, sanctioned by the title «international contest,» given it for the first time by the FIA (Fédération Internationale de l'Automobile). Toyota entered the improved Toyota 7 with a 4,968 cc, V8 engine, with four valves per cylinder, capable of delivering 530 hp and with a top speed of 199 mph (320 km/h). The driver on that occasion was Vic Elford. The rival Nissan, who had already fitted a new, original 12-cylinder, 5-liter engine to the chassis of the R381, increased the displacement of the final version (R382) to 5,954 cc, giving a power of 600 hp and a speed of 217 mph (350 km/h). Isuzu for its part entered an R7 with a Chevrolet V8 engine, while the round-up on national Sports Prototypes was completed by a 1.5-liter Isuzu Bellett, and EVA 2B Can-Am with a 1.3-liter Honda engine and a Fujitsubo Rotary Spider, equipped with a Mazda 982 cc rotary engine. An impressive group of vehicles arrived from Europe to compete on the Fuji circuit, of which the Porsche 917 of Sif-

A Datsun 2000 Sport achieved 1st, 2nd and 4th places in the «D» class on the Daytona speedway in 1970.

fert and Piper and the 908 of Herrmann were outstanding, while Mike Hailwood drove a McLaren M12 Can-Am. Other Porsches, Cobras and Lotuses driven by local competitors completed the list. The winner was the Nissan R382 driven by Motoharu Kurosawa at an average of 175 mph (281 km/h) over the 447 miles (720 km) course. Japan, who was not to compete abroad in the Sports Prototype category for some time yet (essentially at the end of a successful life cycle), nonetheless succeeded with this victory in attracting once more the attention of the international sporting world, which had just witnessed the passage of the Honda comet in the Formula One World Championship.

The Isuzu R7, shown here right competing at the Japanese Grand Prix of 1969, had a 5-liter Chevrolet V8 450 hp engine and Hewland 5-speed transmission.

The Nissan R 381 no. 21 which won the 1969 Japanese Grand Prix had an original 6-liter 12-cylinder capable of developing 600 hp.

The «Toyota 7» of 1970 was driven by a 5-liter V8 turbocharger engine capable of delivering 530 hp.

Japan in Formula One and Two

Honda in Formula One

Following their great successes in the field of motorcycle racing, Honda aroused tremendous interest with their Formula One program which was begun in 1962 and manifested to European enthusiasts with the first tests in July 1964 on the Zandvoort circuit in Holland. The véhicle used in a series of tests on that occasion was a third version, developed from the experience acquired with two earlier prototypes. The first had used a Cooper tubular spaceframe, modified to house the V12 Japanese transverse engine; the second had been the fruit of an original Honda

The Honda F1 team, managed by Yoshio Nakamura, which first competed in the 1964 season, entered two American drivers in 1965: Bucknum and Ginther, seen here at Montecarlo with the numbers 20 and 19, respectively. The Honda V12 transverse engine fed by 6 Keihin twin carburetors (the 1964 version is shown here) was combined with Honda 6-speed transmission.

Ginther's RA-273 during the 1966 Italian Grand Prix. After coming seventh in trials, the American driver retired at the 17th lap following an accident.

project. The final RA-270 version used a central monocoque body in aluminum, with a rear tubular subframe as support for the engine, six-speed gearbox and suspension. Another original feature of the Japanese single-seater, apart from the transverse engine, was the fitting of the front and rear springs-dampers «in-board.» The fuel tanks were situated in the lateral recesses of the monocoque structure. The 1,498 cc engine with its 12- 60 degree V cylinders, fed by six Keihin twin-barrel carburetors, had four valves per cylinder. It had a range of 8,500 to 12,000 rpm, with a maximum of just over 200 hp. For its debut at the German Grand Prix, which took place in the rain at Nürburgring on August 2 the Honda F1 was driven by the Californian Ronnie Bucknum, who was mainly chosen for commercial reasons (exports of the little S 600's to the United States were just beginning). At this first contest, it qualified for the last row on the grid and retired from the race following a minor accident at the 12th lap. In the second and final appearance for 1964 at the Italian Grand Prix, the tiny carburetors were replaced by an injection system. Performance was improved, and it came tenth in trials, but during the race the brakes failed at the 13th lap, to Honda's disappointment. The new RA-272 version of 1965 developed 230 hp at 11,000 rpm according to the manufacturers. Bucknum was joined by another American, the more experienced Ritchie

Ginther, and results began to be more encouraging. Ginther was very fast in trials and after coming sixth in Belgium and Holland, the great day finally arrived. Ginther gave Honda its first Grand Prix victory on the Mexico City circuit on October 24, his team-mate finishing fifth. Unfortunately, this was the last event of the 1,500 cc Formula. By unexpectedly doubling the top limit for engine displacement for the following season, the FIA forced Honda to start again from scratch, directly after they had achieved the desired competitiveness. But the Japanese did not lose heart and set to work on a new vehicle which, entrusted to the same drivers as the previous year, succeeded in coming fourth in Mexico with «Old Ginther» at the wheel. The engine of the RA-273, designed by Irimagiri, was a 12-cylinder, fitted longitudinally. It had a displacement of 2,992 cc and a power of 400 hp, one of the highest for the period. Both the injection system and five-speed gearbox were made by Honda. For 1967, it was decided to enter a single vehicle with John Surtees, who had left Ferrari the previous year following a divorce scandal and taken over from Ginther. The opening in South Africa was very promising, with a good third place, but this was followed by a long series of retirements, interrupted by sixth place in the British Grand Prix and fourth in the German Grand Prix. Weight, bulk and fuel consumption were the biggest enemies of the Japanese vehi-

The victorious RA-300 of Surtees during the 1967 Italian Grand Prix, next to Amon's Ferrari; the British driver snatched victory from Brabham's Brabham-Repco at an average of 140 mph (226 km/h).

Surtees came fourth at the 1968 Belgian Grand Prix, in the RA-301.

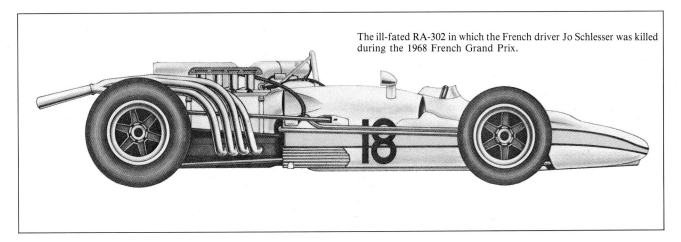

The ill-fated RA-302 in which the French driver Jo Schlesser was killed during the 1968 French Grand Prix.

cle. The new RA-300, developed by Eric Broadley with important contributions from Surtees himself, was first seen in Italy. The chassis of the new car, a central monocoque body with an auxiliary front and rear tube structure, was built in Britain and derived from that used on the Indy version of the Lola. The Monza Grand Prix was one of the most exciting in the history of motor racing, the outcome only being decided at the last curve, the «Parabolica,» where Surtees and Jack Brabham were playing cat and mouse when victory was seized by the driver of the Honda, who won by barely half a length. The RA-300 then ended its career by coming fourth at the last traditional appointment in Mexico. For the 1968 season, Honda substantially modified its V12, putting the air inlet, where the 12 exhaust pipes had been, these being shifted to either side of the engine and passing beneath the suspension. The stated power of the new RA-301 was 450 hp, while the weight was considerably reduced. The characteristics of this single-seater made it particularly suitable for the fastest circuits, as shown by the achievement of a record lap speed of over 150 mph (241 km/h), on average at Spa and pole-position in Monza. But the results for the year were somewhat disappointing, apart from a good second place in France, a fifth in Great Britain and a third in the United States.

Also in 1968, a highly ambitious project had been completed which led to the development of one of the most advanced single-seater of all time: the RA-302. The monocoque body was in fact built of magnesium and the chassis was drawn in at the rear to form a single support beam member for the engine, transmission and suspension. The 380 hp 8- 120 degree V8 engine was unique in the history of 3,000 cc Formula One engines in that it was air-cooled. The first appearance of the new single-seater, which took place at the French Grand Prix, was really premature for the vehicle's state of advancement, which Surtees himself pronounced as inadequate. On 7 July at Rouen, the machine was driven in the rain by the inexperienced Jo Schlesser, a Formula Two driver who, having qualified for entry by coming second to last, skidded off the race track at the third lap. The car immediately burst into flames, mainly due to the inflammability of the magnesium chassis, killing the driver. The controversy surrounding the tragedy aroused was a source of great concern to the top management of Honda. The RA-302, this time with an aluminum monocoque body, was only entered once more at Monza. With the British driver David Hobbs at the wheel, it retired at the 40th lap. Meanwhile, however, plans to withdraw from racing had been gaining ground and the decision was taken at the end of the season.

Dominion in Formula Two

Honda's international activity had not been confined to Formula One racing during the sixties. The company achieved greater success in Formula Two in 1965 and 1966, the last of the 1,000 cc races. At that time, it was normal

The final appearance of Honda in F1 in the sixties was with Bonnier's RA-301 at the 1968 Mexican Grand Prix.

In the 1985 season, the Williams-Honda FW-10, driven by Rosberg (in the photo) and Mansell won four of the sixteen Grand Prix events.

for there to be many crack racing drivers in the B-grade Formula, and interest in this championship was considerable. Honda entrusted its own engine, for which Ron Tauranac built a special chassis, to Brabham. The engine in question was a 1-liter, 4-cylinder twin-shaft with Lucas mechanical injection and a respectable 139 hp. In the first year of the Anglo-Japanese partnership, Jack Brabham had no great success, mainly due to the lack of power of the Honda engine at low speeds, with the result that six-speed gearbox developed. It was in 1966 that the Brabham-Honda permitted its drivers, Brabham and Denny Hulme to monopolize the entire season thanks to a distinct improvement in the power delivered by the engine, enabling them to finish first and second. Following the change in regulations in 1967, Honda decided to give up their F2 program and concentrate on the F1, which was in fact less successful. Having interrupted their activity in the Grand Prix as well, a Honda-engined single-seater was only seen again in 1980.

In that year, in fact, the company entrusted one of its own engines to the Ralt team of Ron Tauranac, with Nigel Mansell as leading driver.

The new Formula Two Ralt-Honda RT-20 had a 1,990 cc V6 engine capable of delivering about 300 hp at 10,500 rpm. The results did not do justice to the vehicle's potential, which was better fulfilled the following year when Geoff Lees won the European championship. In 1982 the 6-cylinder Honda engine of Johansson and Boutsen's Ralt proved itself the best of the bunch again, even if the vehicle was not sufficiently competitive overall to prevent the title going to the rival March-BMW. However, the Ralt-Honda soon took its revenge, winning in the 1983 and 1984 seasons, with Palmer and Thackwell, respectively, after which Formula Two made for the F.3000.

Return to the Grand Prix

At the beginning of the eighties, Formula One vehicles were in a state of transition from 3,000 cc aspirated engines to 1,500 cc turbos. Honda thus had every reason to develop a supercharged version of its excellent 6-cylinder. The new RA-163-E 1,499 cc engine which had an 80 degree Vee, underwent a series of tests in Japan, followed by a 1983 season of trials and development. For this purpose it was entrusted to a smaller stable, the Spirit Racing company of John Wickham. The first version of the new engine had a cast iron cylinder block; supercharging was by means of two KKK turbines. The Spirit-Honda 201 had its debut at the British Grand Prix at Silverstone, where the new vehicle, driven by Stefan Johansson, finished 14th in trials but withdrew during the race. The best result of the season was a 7th place won by the Swedish driver in Holland. It was obvious that the potential of the

Nelson Piquet in the Williams-Honda FW-11 during the 1986 San Marino Grand Prix.

Honda could only be fully realized by an outstanding team and an agreement was drawn up with Williams, who had just won the World Championship with Keke Rosberg. In the final test of the season at Kyalami, the new Williams-Honda FW-09 thus entered the race and, with the Finnish driver at the wheel, achieved a promising fifth place. For 1984, Frank Williams' team was composed of Rosberg again and Jacques Laffite. The former opened the season with a good second place in Brazil, going on to win two fourth places in Belgium and France. A chassis that was inadequate for the power of the new engine, which was now equipped with more suitable IHI turbines but still subject to some teething troubles, prevented it from being consistently competitive, despite the fact that Rosberg's Williams-Honda managed to beat Arnoux's Ferrari at the Grand Prix which took place in the city of Dallas in July: a well-earned victory, backed up by Laffite in fourth place. This success, however, was followed by a long series of retirements which could not be limited even by the improved FW-09B which was entered from the Austrian Grand Prix onward. The marriage of the British chassis and Japanese engine involved certain adaptations, followed by a period of joint development which began to give good results from the 1985 season onward. The new FW-10 designed by Patrick Head combined excellent stability with a power which, given the wildly varying data of the turbo, was in all probability the highest of any of the competitors, even if not sufficient to trou-

ble the unbeatable McLaren-Porsche beyond a certain point. In the course of a year characterized by a continual escalation in power (about 850 hp for the best engines in the competition version) and in spite of tighter limits on fuel consumption, the Williams owed much of its success to the improved engine introduced by Honda in June 1985, which had a better bore-stroke ratio and employed sophisticated materials above all for the pistons and connecting rods.

The number of horsepower delivered varied from approximately 760 to 960, depending on the pressure of supercharging used (from 3.5 to 4.5 atmospheres). The Williams-Honda was thus able to secure four victories, two with Rosberg in Detroit and in the Australian Grand Prix which closed the season, and two with Mansell in the European Grand Prix at Brands Hatch and in South Africa. In the final reckoning, the Finnish driver came third behind Prost and Alboreto, while his team-mate finished sixth behind Senna and De Angelis. In the space of three years, Honda thus succeeded in winning a position in the vanguard of the Formula One sector. Such a result was largely due to first-rate organization, a precise program of work and a spirit of technical cooperation within the team which was very different from the reliance on individual «genius» typical of the European school. These qualities, combined with an advanced technological base in terms of electronics and new materials, have earned the Honda a «name» in the history of motor racing.

Rallies
and Long-Distance Races

Ever since the 1950s, the Japanese industry had understood the commercial importance of long-distance road races, using vehicles which were much closer in appearance to their normal types of automobile production. Their promotional value was first demonstrated to Nissan after the success of the little Datsun 210 in its category in the Australian Rally. But participation in rallies of international importance on a level with their more mature European competitors did not occur until the seventies, above all after the institution of the Rally International Championship in 1970 (renamed Rally World Championship in 1973) increased the recognition of this type of competition. The first to win the honors in this event was the Datsun 240Z, which drew on the experience acquired with the earlier 1600 responsible for the company's first official success in the East African Safari of 1970. The 240Z Fairlady was a thoroughbred grand touring car in appearance too, with a 2.4-liter, 6-cylinder 230 hp engine, which in the racing version had three twin-barrel carburetors, instead of the normal two. It was too large and heavy to try and compete with the Alpines, Lancias and Porsches in the classic European rallies but succeeded nonetheless in winning a very good fifth place at Montecarlo with Aaltonen and tenth with Fall in 1971. Its strong points were its great so-

lidity and reliability, which were the keys to its success in the 1971 and 1973 editions of the East African Safari, with Edgar Herrmann and Shekhar Mehta, respectively. The African contest had always been a good battleground for the Japanese cars and the Mitsubishi Lancer 1600 GSR also won the 1974 and 1976 editions, driven on both occasions by Joginder Singh. In the latter year, an important outright victory was achieved by Harry Kallstrom's Datsun Violet at the Acropolis Rally in Greece. Toyota meanwhile had also begun to feature quite prominently in rallies, a notable success being that of the Celica 1600 GT Group 5 in the RAC (Royal Automobile Club) International Rally of 1972. Absolute victory in following years was achieved by the Corolla, namely with Walter Boyce as driver in the Press on Regardless held in the United States in 1973 and with Hannu Mikkola two years later at the Australian South Pacific Rally and Thousand Lakes Rally. From 1979 to 1981, Datsun succeeded in coming second in the World Constructors Class, behind Ford, Fiat and Talbot, respectively, thanks to a series of good placings and a few significant outright victories, like the three consecutive wins of the East African Safari with Mehta's Violet 160J. Timo Salonen also carried a similar vehicle to success in the New Zealand Rally in 1980

Left, the Datsun 2000 Sport at Montecarlo in 1968; right, the Celica 1600 GT Group 5 in the Royal Automobile Club International Rally of 1972.

and won the Ivory Coast Rally with a Violet GT in 1981. The following year the era of four-wheel drive began for rallies, the new Audi Quattro winning the world championship. Datsun secured a good third place which was achieved once again thanks to the victory of Mehta in the Safari, driving a Violet GT. Also in 1982, Waldegaard's Toyota Celica won the Ivory Coast Rally. In 1983, the new Group B vehicles developed by Nissan and Toyota appeared. The first had its debut at Montecarlo, where it came 14th with the Salonen-Harjanne team. This was the 240 RS, derived from the Silvia series model. The 2,340 cc 16-valve 4-cylinder engine was capable of delivering about 280 hp at 8,000 rpm, which was not a lot, considering the quality of the other competitors. In that year's Safari, the engines of both Salonen, who was in charge of the event, and Mehta, proved somewhat fragile, forcing Nissan to withdraw. The Toyota Team Europe (TTE) directed by Ove Andersson made a more promising start. At the beginning of the 1983 RAC Rally, the new Celica Group B won a good seventh place with Kankkunen-Pironen, later managing with Waldegaard to beat Mikkola's Audi Quattro in the Ivory Coast rally. The success of the Japanese vehicles in the African races was largely due to their hardiners, which was more important on such roads than the technical refinements of their European rivals. But there were other reasons. The Celica used a 2,090 cc 4-cylinder engine capable of delivering between 320 and 360 hp thanks to the KKK turbosupercharger and Nippondenso electronic injection system. The 1984 season signaled the entry of the TTE into the African Safari. It was a triumphant debut. It was in fact Waldegaard who won the race with his Toyota, leaving the Opel Manta 400 of Aaltonen, Audi Quattro of Mikkola, Lancia Rally of Alen and Nissan 240 RS of Mehta behind him, in that order. The success of the Toyota was largely due to great regularity, enviable reliability, good power and speed and excellent Pirelli tires. A recipe for success which was improved still further in 1985 when the Celicas won first and second positions with Kankkunen and Waldegaard respectively their compatriot Nissan 240-RS, driven by Kirkland, being relegated to third place. The positive year of 1985 also ended with a new, dual victory in the Ivory Coast with Kankkunen finishing in front of his team-mate Waldegaard. But it was Nissan who preceded Toyota's fourth place in the world championship, thanks to good positions in the Acropolis, New Zealand and Argentinian rallies.

In the eighties, Mitsubishi has also carried on its own program of participation in major rallies, both in the context of the Rally World Championship, in which a Lancer EX 2000 won third place in the Thousand Lakes rally of 1982 and in special contests like the Pharaohs' Rally and the Paris-Dakar. In the Egyptian race, a Chariot 4WD came first for its category. In 1984, while the list of results obtained by the Pajero in the great Euro-African long-distance races is longer. In 1983 and 1984, it came first in its class, while in 1985, Zaniroli-Da Silva's Mitsubishi was the overall winner, backed up by the Cowan-Syer team in second place.

Above, the Datsun 240Z which came third at the 1972 Montecarlo Rally. Below, the Mitsubishi Colt Lancer of J. Singh and D. Doig which won the East African Safari in 1974.

Above, the Nissan 280 ZX of 1974. Below the Nissan Violet which won the 1980 East African Safari and right, the Mazda RX-4 which took part in the London-Sydney Rally.

The turbocharged Toyota Celica which came sixth in the 1982 Thousand Lakes Rally.

After the successes of 1984 and 1985, the Toyota Celica Twin Cam Turbo also won the 1986 edition of the East African Safari, with the Waldegaard/Gallagher team (seen left in action).

The Nissan RS 240 produced in 1983 has a 2,340 cc carburetor-fed 16-valve, 4-cylinder engine capable of delivering about 280 hp.

The Mazda 323 Turbo Group A in action at the 1984 Montecarlo Rally with the Warmbold-Feltz team.

The Mazda RX-7 taken during the Swedish Rally on 1985; the best result achieved in this season was sixth position at the Acropolis Rally.

The Mitsubishi Pajero driven by Zaniroli-Da Silva triumphed at the 1985 Paris-Dakar.

Endurance

The Japanese industry could not fail to be present in the endurance contests, although its involvement in this type of competition has been somewhat limited at an international level. Japanese builders in the eighties have mainly concentrated on the American IMSA scenario and a few appearances in European classics like the 24-Hour Le Mans race. The changes in regulations affecting the Constructors World Championship in the last ten years (one only need think of the controversy surrounding the Silhouette Group 5 and later, the limits in fuel consumption introduced with the Group C) have discouraged many companies from involving themselves in contests which have often assumed the appearance of Porsche «monobrands.» The clear separation between the Group C and IMSA championships has also greatly reduced the world significance of a category which was formerly one of the top motor racing events in terms of importance and popularity. The Japanese have thus maintained only tenuous links with these series, even if their Sports Prototype vehicles have become increasingly important in their national events. For IMSA and Group C categories, the Japanese constructors have generally fitted engines of their own design to chassis of European origin.

One of the best results obtained by Japanese vehicles in the endurance contests of the Old World, was the victory of the Mazda 717C in the C Junior category of the 1983 edition of the 24-Hour Le Mans race, this vehicle coming twelfth in the overall results. Driven by the 1,308 cc Wankel 13B twin rotor, capable of delivering about 300 hp at 9,000 rpm, this vehicle with its Japanese drivers Katayama, Terada and Yorino, covered 4,122 km at an average speed of 107 mph (172 km/h), also winning the top «performance rating.»

The Fuji 1,000 km Endurance World Championship of 1985 appeared to be dominated by Japanese cars. A March-Nissan 85G and Nissan 85C in fact secured first and second places, followed by a Toyota 85C, but one must not forget that both the official Porsche 962s which had dominated the trials and other qualified European teams did not undertake the race, owing to the prohibitive weather conditions which in fact caused it to be suspended after barely two hours.

In the IMSA series, the image of the Japanese car is associated above all with the long run of successes achieved in the GT category by the Mazda RX-7, Nissan 280 ZX and 300 ZX and Toyota Celica. But there has been no shortage of interesting prototypes with Japanese engines, such as the Lola-Mazda T616, which had also been seen in Europe, and the Argo-Mazda JM16, both with rotary engines, apart from a few appearances of the Toyota TOM's.

The Mazda GTU at the 1980 IMSA.

The Mazda RX-7 GTU used in the 1980 (left), 1982 (above), 1984 below and 1985 (opposite above) IMSA series. Left, below, the Mazda RX-7 GTO (1983).

Mazda's commitment to the IMSA series was rewarded by the achievement of six consecutive titles in the GTU category, from 1980-1985. After the first victory in this category at Daytona in 1979, the RX-7 went on to win another 60 events up to 1985, to which should be added the six victories in the GTO category. The RX-7 GTU's are fitted with a 12A rotary engine (573 × 2 cc); the GTO has a 13B engine (654 × 2 cc) with powers of 270 hp at 9,000 rpm and 300 hp at 8,500 rpm, respectively. In both cases, lubrication is of the dry sump type.

Above and right are two views of the 1985 Nissan 300 ZX Turbo of the Bob Sharp Racing team used in the GTO category. Equipped with a 2.9-liter V6 engine, it was driven by the filmstar/racing driver Paul Newman. The 5-speed transmission is by Weismann.

Above, the Nissan GTP ZX Turbo, one of the protagonists of the 1985 IMSA series. The engine, which is based on the V6 of the 300 ZX, is a supercharged 2,960 cc capable of delivering 650 hp at 8,000 rpm. Below, the 1985 versions of the DOME'S Toyota (left) and the TOM'S Toyota Group C, with a 2,090 cc engine with double turbocharger delivering 503 hp. A TOM's Toyota came twelfth overall in the 1985 24-Hour Le Mans race.

Above, the Nissan Silvia Group C of 1985, based on the modified March 85 G chassis and equipped with the Nissan VG 30 T/C engine, a 2,960 cc V6 supercharged by two turbochargers and with electronic fuel injection, delivering 650 hp at 8,000 rpm. Below, the March-Nissan 85 G, used in both IMSA and Constructors World Championships. Bottom the TOM'S Toyota of 1985.

Mazda has achieved flattering successes at Le Mans with the rotary-engined C2's. Above, the 717 C (13B engine with Bosch Kugelfisher injection) which came twelfth overall and first in its class in 1983; below, the technically similar 727 C, which came tenth overall and first in its class the following year. Right, the 737 C of 1985 (with carburetor fuel feed and a longer wheelbase).

The Argo-Mazda RGP 500 with a 13B engine used in the 1985 IMSA series (above). The Lola T616 with a Mazda 13B engine, in action at the 1984 24-Hour Daytona race (below).

FROM 1907
TO THE PRESENT

Daihatsu

Daihatsu, which figures eighth in the Japanese car industry line-up, became part of the Toyota group in 1967. Production (partly integrated with the mother company's) includes a series of mid-size segment vehicles, off-road models, and light commercial vehicles.

Production rates in the first half of the 1980s were roughly between 130,000 and 185,000, to which should be added those vehicles assembled under Toyota, approximately 140,000. Exports accounted for around 45 percent in 1981, and 34 percent in 1983. Daihatsu represents about 2.3 percent of total Japanese production, and 2.5 percent of exports, with a total turnover (1984) of 470 billion yen. The company has not developed spectacularly, its production policy seeking to maintain its well established niche in the sector of small economy cars. Founded in 1907, it originally manufactured internal combustion engines. The

year 1930 saw the first motor vehicle, a small three wheeled motor vehicle which was to be the mainstay of the company for over 20 years. Overseas exports started in 1957 with another three-wheeled called the Tri-Mobile.

Then in 1958 appeared the Bee, the first car, a three-wheel, four-door sedan, with a 540 cc air-cooled rear-mounted engine. Only a few of these were made, however, and in 1963 the Compagno became the first Daihatsu vehicle to come regularly off the production line. With four wheels it looked less unusual, and the engine was 4-cylinder, 797 cc, increasing to 958 cc in 1965 with the 1000 a 2- or 4-door sedan that also sold as a station-wagon.

The Fellow (2-cylinder, 2-stroke, 356 cc) came on the market in 1966, but was completely redesigned in 1970 and named Fellow Max.

In 1974 a middle range sedan, was introduced, the Char-

Compagno. Daihatsu's first standard production-line car, the Compagno came out first in 1963. Available as a sedan (left), station-wagon, or sports car (right), it had a water-cooled engine, 4 cylinders in line (797 cc, 41 hp at 5,000 rpm). In 1965 the cylinder capacity was increased to 958 cc (55 hp at 5,500 rpm for the sedan, and 65 for the sports version, with a twin-barrel carburetor). Both had synchronized 4-speed gears, while the respective maximum speeds were 81 and 90 mph (130 - 145 km/h). Rear-wheel drive. Suspension: rigid rear axle with semielliptic leafsprings.

Fellow/Fellow Max. The little Fellow (left), brought out in 1966, had a water-cooled, twin-cylinder two-stroke engine (356 cc, 23 hp JIS at 5,000 rpm). Max. speed 62 mph (100 km/h). A station-wagon version was also available. Appearing in 1970 under the name Fellow Max (right), the second series was completely redesigned, with new sedan and coupé bodies. The twin-cylinder engine, developed 31 to 37 hp according to the model. Mechanically the changes included front-wheel drive and four-wheel independent suspension. Fully synchronized 4-speed gears.

121

Consorte. In 1969 the Compagno was replaced by the Consorte, which retained the classic format of front-engine and rear-wheel drive. Engines: water-cooled, 4-cylinder, 958 cc and 1,166 cc (developed first by Toyota), 58 and 64 hp respectively, max. speed 87 and 93 mph (140-150 km/h). Independent front suspension with rigid rear axle and semielliptic leafsprings. The more powerful model had disc brakes at the front. Gears: initially 4-speed, then optional 5-speed on the 1.2-liter models, or 2-shift Toyota Toyo-Glide automatic transmission with hydraulic converter. A five-seat coupé body is also available in the Consorte range, with the same mechanical specifications.

Charmant. Broadening the top end of the Daihatsu range, the Charmant came out in December 1974. A classic rear-wheel drive sedan (above) based on the Toyota Corolla, it came in two versions, both 4-cylinder, 1,166 and 1,407 cc (64 and 86 hp). Gears were 4- or 5-speed, or alternatively the Toyota 2-shift automatic gearbox. The suspension was the same as on the Consorte. Brakes: disc at the front (if requested), drum at the back. Available with two or four doors, or as a five-door station-wagon. All Toyota engines, including the new 1,290 and 1,588 cc (72 and 88 hp respectively) introduced in 1978. In 1981 the Charmant was restyled (below) and a new range of engines brought out (1,290, 1,452, 1,576 cc).

mant, with 4 cylinders, 1.2- and 1.4-liter. Between 1976 and 1977 production was boosted by the Cuore, a small three- or five-door economy car with front-wheel drive, with a twin-cylinder 547 cc engine, and the Charade with a new 3-cylinder 993 cc engine (55 hp at 5,500 rpm). After a sharp drop following the oil crisis, sales picked up again to 123,233 in 1978 (16.1 percent for export). That year Daihatsu was 28th in the world league of car manufacturers, after Volvo but before Suzuki. In the first half of the 1980s production centered on the Cuore (reintroduced in 1980), the Charade (a new model in 1983), and the Charmant.

Cuore/Mira. Developed from the Fellow Max, the small Cuore first appeared in 1976 (left), powered by a new 2-cylinder four-stroke water-cooled engine (547 cc, 28 hp at 6,000 rpm), with a maximum speed of 68 mph (110 km/h). With totally restyled bodywork in 1980 (below, left), the range (also called Mira) was expanded to include a version with turbocharger (41 hp at 6,000 rpm) capable of up to 81 mph (130 km/h). For certain markets the cylinder capacity was raised to 617 cc. The gears were either 4- or 5-speed, or 2-shift automatic. Of particular interest was the version with four-wheel drive switching to the rear wheels. The third Cuore/Mira series (below) came out in 1985 with (for certain markets) a 3-cylinder 840 cc engine (44 hp at 5,500 rpm). Bodywork: either three or five doors.

Charade. The first Charade sedan (above, left) appeared in 1977, the coupé (above, right) following in 1978. The engine was a specially designed 3-cylinder, 993 cc, 50 or 55 hp at 5,500 rpm, with a max. speed of 87 mph (140 km/h). Variants of this engine appeared in the new series in 1983 (below, left), with the basic version being raised to 60 hp. The Charade De Tomaso Turbo is supercharged (80 hp at 5,500 rpm); two diesel models with the same cylinder capacity also came out at this time (38 hp suction and 50 hp turbo). For some export markets the whole series was increased to 986 cc (between 52 and 68 hp for the gasoline versions, and 37 and 46 hp for the diesel). In 1985 it received a general facelift (below, right).

Taft. Brought out in 1975, the Taft (F-10) at first had a 4-cylinder in line (958 cc), with an alternative 1,587 cc (66 hp at 4,800 rpm) F20 model coming out the next year and subsequently replacing it. The F50 2,530 cc diesel engine (62 hp at 3,600 rpm) came out in 1978, to be superseded in 1982 by the F60 (2,765 cc, 69 hp at the same rpm rate). The chassis had box-section ladder frame; front and rear suspension: rigid axle, with longitudinal leafsprings and telescopic dampers; 4-speed gears with reducer. Front disc brakes available on request, and four-wheel drive switching to the front wheels.

Rocky. With 4-cylinder 1,998 cc (88 hp at 4,600 rpm) gasoline fueled or 2,765 cc (73 hp) Toyota diesel engines, the F80 and F70 (or F75) respectively, the Rocky replaced the Taft in 1984. Similar in both chassis and body to the Toyota Blizzard, its main features are rigid axle suspension both front and back, and 3-position electronically adjustable hydraulic dampers; 5-speed gears with transfer box ratio; four-wheel drive incorporating a rear limited slip differential. Disc brakes at the front. Available either as canvas top convertible (above), hardtop (right), stationwagon, or long-wheelbase station-wagon.

Several important agreements for cooperation were also reached internationally. In 1980 China recreated a factory for light commercial vehicles (the Tianjin Automobile Industry Corp.), with a contract for Daihatsu to supply components for 5,000 vehicles a year. Then in 1981 the Italian firm Innocenti (part of the De Tomaso group) used the Daihatsu 3-cylinder 993 cc engine, and in 1983 also the diesel version, for its Mini. In June 1984 a triennial contract was concluded to supply 27,000 engines and technology relating to turbocharger and bodywork design. Another Italian company, Alfa Romeo, now builds the Charade in its South African factory for the local market.

HiJet/Delta/Atrai. HiJet (also called Atrai for exportation market) and Delta models are light truck/microbus commercial vehicles, similar to the Toyota Lite-Ace series. Three-or four-cylinder, gasoline and diesel engines.

Honda

The biggest motorcycle manufacturer in the world, and the fourth largest Japanese motor vehicle company, Honda only started making cars in 1963, 15 years after the company was set up. In 1948, at the small Hamamatsu factory, Soichiro Honda made a two-stroke 50 cc engine that first featured the little two-wheeler Dream. In 1949 came the first complete motorcycle, and in 1952 the first exports, but it was with the Super Cab in 1958 that Honda really began to make its mark on the growing Japanese motor industry, and the following year saw the creation of a solid American market with the setting up of the «American Honda Motor Co.»

It was through racing that cars evolved as they did. With all the necessary know-how in the field of small four-stroke engines, and inside knowledge of the international market, Honda's first car (1962) combined advanced technology with low consumption and better than average exhaust filtering. The S500 was no ordinary sports car: rather over nine feet (3 m) in length, it had cylinder capacity of barely 531 cc, developing 44 hp at 8,000 rpm. Indicative of its inspiration in motorcycle design, was the separate chain final drive (one for each driving wheel). A coupé version was brought out, after which the cylinder capacity was raised to 606 cc (S600) in 1963, developing 57 hp at 8,500 rpm. The 4-cylinder Honda engine in these small sports cars was very advanced: monobloc and light alloy head, chain-driven twin camshaft distribution, four Keihin carburetors.

Honda's first venture into the car market received excellent publicity through participation in the Formula 1 world championship. The single seater entered for the 1964 German Grand Prix attracted considerable interest, for its transverse engine (V-12 cylinders, 1.5 liters, 215 hp), transistorized ignition and 12 carburetors fuel supply, replaced the following season by a system of indirect injection. Behind the choice of American drivers like Ronnie Bucknum and Ritchie Ginther were commercial considerations. Ginther won the first victory in the 1965 Mexico Grand Prix, the last of the 1.5-liter formulas, succeeded by engines with double cylinder capacity. Honda F.1 cars continued with mixed results until 1968, with only one other victory, a magnificent win at Monza in 1966 with John Surtees at the wheel. During this period a program of Formula 2 cars was also developed.

At first Honda cars were not well received on the home market. In 1966 they had sunk to 0.35 percent penetration. However, the range was substantially renewed that year, and sales picked up. In the sports range came the S800 sports car and coupé with more conventional transmission with final hipoid bevel, and a 791 cc engine (70

S500, S600, S800. Honda entered the realm of car manufacturing in 1962 with the S500, a small sports car that was clearly developed from motorcycle engineering (e.g. two-chain final drive). The 4-cylinder 531 cc engine (44 hp at 8,000 rpm) had four-carburetor and two overhead camshafts. The chassis had box-type ladder frame with tubular cross members, with independent suspension on all four wheels. Max. speed 85mph (137 km/h). Also available as a coupé (below), the Honda Sport S600 (above) was brought out in 1963 (606 cc, 57 hp, 90 mph, 145 km/h), to be followed in 1966 by the S800 (791 cc, 70 hp, 100 mph, 161 km/h), which featured among other things hipoid bevel final drive.

N360, N600. The N360 (above) appeared in 1966. Powered by a four-stroke twin-cylinder 354 cc engine (31 hp at 8,500 rpm), this small front-wheel drive economy car had a maximum speed of 71 mph (115 km/h). Also worth noting about the engine is that it was air-cooled and had a single overhead camshaft. The standard gearbox was 4-speed, but a 3-speed automatic version with torque convertor was also available. For the export market there was the N500 (500 cc, 40 hp at 8,500 rpm), and later the N400 (401 cc, 33 hp at 8,000 rpm) and the N600 (598 cc, 45 hp at 7,000 rpm). In length the vehicle was a bare 9.92 ft, 3.025 m (the N600, 10.1 ft, 3.1 m).

1300. Extremely advanced for its time (1968), the front-wheel drive 1300 had a 4-cylinder 1,298 cc engine (100 hp SAE at 7,000 rpm). One of its features was the first two-way air-cooling system, the «Duo Dyna»; the outside air-cooled the outer walls, and a fan sucked air in through an intake funnel and blew it through a network of ducts in the interior of the engine. Max. speed 109 mph (175 km/h). Integral chassis, independent suspension on all four wheels, and front disc brakes; 4-speed synchromesh gears, or 3-shift automatic. In 1970 a coupé model (below) came out, in two versions, 100 hp (coupé 7) and 116 hp (coupé 9), the latter with a maximum speed of 112 mph (180 km/h).

Z, Life. With 354 or 598 cc twin-cylinder air-cooled engines, the Z series (above) came out in 1970, broadening the range of Honda super economy cars. Originally launched as a coupé, the more powerful of these models (38 hp at 6,600 rpm) had servo front disc brakes and 5-speed fully synchronized gearbox.
Brought out in 1971, the Life 360 (below) had a 2-cylinder water-cooled engine (356 cc, 30 hp at 8,000 rpm); it came with either three or five doors; independent front suspension and rear rigid axle.

Civic/Ballade. Launched in 1972 (above left) the Civic placed Honda firmly among the world's leading car manufacturers. Its international appeal is clear from the number of different models available. For Japan and the United States the engine mounted was a 1,169 cc stratified charge (CVCC system) model with three valves per cylinder, producing 60 hp SAE at 5,500 rpm. For European exports a more conventional type was used, varying between 66 and 72 hp SAE. In 1973 a 1,488 cc engine was introduced, producing 63 hp SAE at 5,500 rpm (CVCC version) or 73 hp at the same rate (ordinary head version). Front-wheel drive with transverse engine, fully independent suspension (McPherson on both axles); 4-speed synchromesh gears, or 2-shift automatic. Available with either three or five doors. Various modifications were made in 1979 (above) including general enlargement of the body and improved rear suspension. In place of the old 1,200 engine, the Civic (above) now mounted a 1,335 cc model developing 68 hp (SAE), 56 hp (SAE Net), and 60 hp (DIN) for the Japanese, American, and European markets respectively. The corresponding capacity of the 1,488 cc version was 80 hp (SAE), 64 (SAE Net), and 70 hp (DIN). Completing the Civic range are the sedan Ballade (left) and the station-wagon.

hp, 100 mph, 161 km/h). But the greatest innovation were the N360 and the N500, small economy front-wheel drive cars with twin-cylinder transverse engine, and the subsequent N400 and N600.

After 1963, when a mere 136 vehicles were built, production rose to 5,210 in 1964, and 8,779 in 1965 (of which almost 25 per cent was exported). In 1966 it sank back to 3,209, of which 60 percent was exported. The new economy car, somewhat similar to the English (Issigonis) «Mini», transformed the company's fortunes: in 1967 more than 87,000 vehicles were produced, and the following year, thanks largely to a spectacular recovery on the home market, production rose to 186,560. The export pattern meanwhile changed: of over 232,000 vehicles built in 1969, exports accounted for a mere 5.4 percent.

The decade ended with the presentation at the 1968 Tokyo Motor Show of the 1300 (alias 77), a four-door sedan with sophisticated technology such as air-cooled engine and dry sump lubrication. Its 100 hp at 7,000 rpm rose to 116 hp at 7,300 rpm in the coupé version brought out two years later. Honda production rose steadily in the early 1970s, with exports also rising (27% of almost 257,000 in 1973). The success of these years was mostly due to the new Civic brought out in 1972 and supplied for the home and American markets with a fuel system with three valves per cylinder, known as «CVCC» (Compound Vortex Controlled Combustion). This design fitted in with the strict antipollution regulations introduced in the United States in 1975. By 1973 the Civic had become the first Honda car to be regularly exported to the United States. Between then and 1979 production grew steadily, rising to 706,375, 76% of which was exported, mostly to the USA, at which market production and commercial strategy had been specifically aimed. This performance has made Honda a symbol of aggressiveness and competitiveness in world trade. The turnover in the car sector exceeded that in the motorcycle sector for the first time in 1976.

Among the new models introduced in the 1970s it is worth mentioning the small Z (1970) and Life (1971), which evolved from the twin-cylinder N line, and the new Accord/Prelude line brought out in 1976, with 1.6- and 1.8-liter models.

Policy in the 1980s was concerned with further developing exports, and with production abroad in those countries where penetration was restricted by government intervention, or where there was opportunity for negotiation with the Japanese industry. Particularly significant here was the agreement with British Leyland drawn up in December 1979 for production under license of the Ballade, rechristened Triumph Acclaim. This took effect in October 1981. The complete overhaul of the Civic/Ballade range in 1983 also affected the new English model, and 1985 saw the appearance of the Rover 200. In 1985-1986 came the two large sedans (the Honda Legend and the Rover 800) built in Japan for the home and Asian markets, and in Britain for the European market. In the United States meanwhile Honda and Rover cars continued to compete. In 1982 the Marysville (Ohio) factory opened for assembly of the Accord range. Representing an investment of 250 million dollars, this factory can produce 150,000 ve-

Accord/Vigor/Prelude. The first series of Accords came out in May 1976, in a three-door hatchback version (above), followed in October of the next year by a four-door sedan (top), and then in November 1978 by the Prelude coupé (below). Front-wheel drive, with fully independent suspension, these cars had a 4-cylinder 1,599 cc engine (80 hp SAE at 5,300 rpm), modified when the Prelude was launched to 1,602 cc (80 hp DIN for the European market and 69 hp SAE Net for the American and Japanese CVCC versions). In October 1978 there also came out a 1,750 cc CVCC (90 hp SAE) model (73 hp SAE for the USA).

Quint/Quintet/Quint Integra. The Quint, a five-door hatchback was launched in 1980. With a 4-cylinder 1,602 cc injection engine (90 hp JIS at 5,300 rpm, and 80 hp for the European export model Quintet), it had a maximum speed of 103 mph (165 km/h). In February 1985 the new Quint Integra came out: a three-door hatchback with a new 1,590 cc engine (four valves per cylinder, 115 hp, or 135 hp with injection).

Accord/Prelude. The second series of Accords came out in October 1981 (under the name Vigor on certain markets), then in November 1982 the new Prelude coupé appeared. Initially supplied with the same engines as the first series, the Accord acquired two new ones (1,598 and 1,830 cc) in 1984, both with CVCC system for the Japanese and American markets. The Prelude had a 1.8-liter engine, though with one model developing 125 hp, 114 mph (183 km/h), incorporating among other features an ALB anti-blocking braking system. In 1983 the sedan and hatchback were slightly restyled. Shown here: the 1981 and 1983 sedans (above, left and right), the 1983 hatchback (left), and the Prelude (below).

hicles yearly, to increase steadily with a target of 400,000 in 1990. Including both imported cars and cars built locally, Honda had captured 5% of the total American market by 1985, with sales exceeding 550,000, 26% of which were built at Marysville.

Automobile production in the first half of the 1980s stayed constant, around 850,000, some 600,000 of which came

Jazz/City. Sold as «City» in Japan and as «Jazz» on certain export markets, this small economy car has a 4-cylinder CVCC engine (1,232 cc) with three valves per cylinder, producing 45 hp (basic model, with 4- or 5-speed manual transmission), 55 hp (with Hondamatic automatic transmission), and 100 or 110 hp (turbocharged, without or with intercooler respectively). First launched in 1981. Dating from 1983, the sports version designed by the Italian designer Pininfarina is marketed only at home, with engines ranging from 63 to 110 hp.

from the Suzuka factory, one of the most up to date in existence. To these should be added the CKD components (77,000 in 1983, 1,139,500 in 1984, 217,000 in 1985) for assembly in the United States, Indonesia, Malaysia, New Zealand, Thailand, and Taiwan, and in the factory shared by Honda and Mercedes-Benz in South Africa, for assembly of vehicles intended for the local market.

The turnover for the 1985 financial year was over 2,650 billion yen, of which cars accounted for 61.1%, motorcycles 16%, and other sectors for the rest.

The latest Honda range is based on the small twin-cylinder Today (brought out in 1985); the City/Jazz, a roomy, economy town car (either convertible or three-door models); the mid-size range Civic/Ballade (available as hatchback, notchback, coupé and space-wagon); the Quint series developed from Accord/Prelude; the Accord, an interesting middle-top range sedan; the coupé Prelude, and the great Legend. Honda produces also the mini-van range «Acty». Mention should also be made of the collaboration with the Italian bodywork designer Pininfarina, who designed the convertible version of the Honda City and developed the HP-X prototype introduced at the 1984 Turin Show.

In the racing world, after a return to Formula 2 in 1980, Honda once again entered the Formula 1 Grand Prix pits with a 6-cylinder supercharged engine in a Spirit (1983), then in a Williams (1984). The results achieved in the Williams-Honda by Rosberg and Mansell in 1985 and Piquet and Mansell in 1986 are a sufficient indication of the high technical level of this Anglo-Japanese venture, and most especially of the remarkable quality of the engine.

Accord/Vigor. Brought out in June 1985, the third series Accord/Vigor comes in sedan notchback (above), three-door hatchback, and (below) «Aerodeck» versions (the latter an original design developed from the 1983 Civic, offering a station-wagon with sportscar style). All transversally mounted, 4-cylinder (12 or 16 valves), the engines vary according to the market. Japanese models have a displacement of 1,829, 1,834, and 1,958 cc (the latter with four valves per cylinder), producing 110, 131 and 160 hp (JIS) respectively. European models are supplied with 1,587 or 1,958 cc engines, 88 hp (DIN) and 106 hp (or 122 hp injection) respectively. For the American market a 1,955 cc (110 hp SAE Net) model is mounted. These cars have highly sophisticated suspension: a more developed variant of the double wishbones type, keeping the wheels in virtually constant alignment in all conditions.

Civic/Ballade. Totally redesigned in 1983, the Civic range includes: a three-door hatchback (above), a four-door sedan (also marketed as Ballade, below), a coupé CR-X (bottom) and a space-wagon Civic Shuttle. Four-cylinder engines with displacement of 1,187, 1,342, 1,488 and 1,590 cc, producing from 55 to 135 hp, and all with three valves per cylinder (a characteristic Honda design). An exception to these is the more powerful 1.6-liter version, with four valves per cylinder. Five-speed gears, or 3-shift automatic. The Shuttle is also available with four-wheel drive. Directly derived from the Ballade is the Rover 200 series produced in Great Britain by Austin Rover.

Today. Both the body design and the engineering of the small Today (launched at the end of 1985) are highly sophisticated. Its most outstanding features include a light alloy 2-cylinder engine, horizontal in line, 545 cc, developing 31 hp at 5,500 rpm. Maximum speed 81 mph (130 km/h); 4-speed transmission, or optional automatic. Front disc brakes.

Legend. Launched at the 1985 Tokyo Motor Show, the Legend was Honda's first venture into the luxury car market. Designed in collaboration with Austin Rover (the same partnership also produced the Rover 800), it comes with two V6 engines with four valves per cylinder, single shaft distribution and electronic injection: one 2-liter model (125 hp), and a 2.5-liter (160 hp JIS) version. Front-wheel drive, and 5-speed gears. The front suspension is the same as on the Accord/Prelude series (double wishbones suspension). The substantial body 15.7 ft (4.81 m) long boasts an aerodynamic coefficient of Cd = 0.32.

Isuzu

In the 1980s «Isuzu Motor Limited» became Japan's third largest manufacturer of industrial vehicles, and the third largest producer of diesel engines in the world. The car sector only accounts for 14% of the turnover (769.1 billion yen in 1984), as against light commercial vehicles (34%), engines (28%), and heavy trucks and buses (24%). The company dates back to 1916, when the Tokyo Ishikawajima Ship Building and Engineering Co. merged with the Tokyo Gas and Electric Industrial Co. to begin automobile production. In 1918 a contract was agreed with the English company Wolseley for exclusive production and marketing rights of Wolseley products in the Far East. Then in December 1922, after four years of experimentation and testing, there appeared the first Japanese-built Wolseley (the A9 Model). In 1929 an independent company was set up (initially called Ishikawajima Automotive Works Co., then Automobile Industries Co.) to make cars, now also to original designs. The trade names used were «Sumida» and «Chiyoda», both subsequently unified to «Isuzu» (after the name of the river). Finally, on April 9, 1937 the «Tokyo Automobile Industries Co.» was created, with a capital of a million yen, and in 1949 the company became definitively «Isuzu Motor Ltd.» Industrial vehicles were the mainstay of production (the first diesel engine — 5.3-liter, air-cooled — appearing in 1936), and despite the large PA10 sedan (1943) car manufacture only really took off after the war, with the agreement with the Roots group reached in February 1953 for production of Hillman cars under license. The first of these came off the Isuzu assembly lines in 1953, and by 1957 the English Minx was a completely Japanese production. Production figures grew gradually between 1956 and 1961, from 2,042 to 10,875, but the leap to over 34,000 in 1964 was due to the launch of cars built to original designs in the new Fujisawa factory (the Bellel in 1961 and the Bellett in 1963). The 1.5-liter four-door Bellel sedan was the

Bellel, Bellett. Production of original Isuzu cars began with the Bellel in 1961 (above), a traditional four-door sedan (engines: 4-cylinder, 1,471 cc, 2-liter diesel, the very first Japanese diesel model).
Two years later came the Bellett (below), with the same engine (1.5-liter, 68 hp, max. speed 90 mph, 145 km/h). The gearbox was 4-speed synchronized or 3-shift automatic. Later engines were 1,584 and 1,817 cc (90 and 94 hp). A two-door coupé body was also available.

Florian. The 1,584 cc Florian was launched at the 1967 Tokyo Motor Show. Preceded the year before by the 117 coupé (below), this sedan was built along similar lines, with bodywork by the Italian designer Ghia. It featured a double overhead camshaft and twin carburetors and was available at either 84 or 103 hp. The later version 1,817 cc sedan and coupé were 100 and 120 hp respectively. The injection 117 EC61 developed 130 hp at 6,600 rpm. In 1977 the Florian range was extended to include a 1,952 cc 62 hp diesel model, with a maximum speed of about 81 mph (130 km/h). The following year also saw a fuel injection 1,950 cc engine (either 120 or 135 hp) for the coupé.

first Japanese car to be offered with a diesel engine too. After the launch of the coupé 117 version in 1966, the Bellel was finally replaced the following year by the new Florian sedan, with a 1.6 liter engine.

In the late sixties and early seventies efforts were made to find a partner to support a development program and general rethink of production (since the models on offer were probably in too high a range for the demands of the Japanese market at that period).

An agreement concluded in 1966 with «Fuji Heavy Industries» lasted only two years, and that with Mitsubishi was even shorter-lived, starting in 1968 and ending in 1969. Nissan then became interested in Isuzu, but the collaboration was hardly any luckier, lasting from March 1970 until a little over a year later. Meanwhile car production had dropped from 39,776 in 1968 to 18,815 in 1970.

The way ahead was cleared in the end with an agreement with General Motors, who in September 1971 took a 34% shareholding in the company. This led to an integration of production and marketing, beginning with exportation of a light truck to the USA. The factories were updated, and even the company logo was completely redesigned in 1974, symbolising a break with the past. The first of the «new blood» cars was the Gemini, a version of the Opel Kadett/Chevrolet Chevette.

The agreement also led to the importation of a certain number of Chevrolet cars into Japan. Isuzu Motors America Inc. was founded in 1975. Now centered on the Gemini and Florian models, production rose from 14,734 in 1973 to 64,735 in 1976, with a rise in exports during the same period from 0.7 per cent to 35.2 per cent. In 1978 102,883 cars were built, of which 53.2 per cent were exported. An interesting and highly sophisticated coupé, the Piazza/Impulse, designed by the Italian Giorgio Giugiaro, came on the market in 1981. The off-road Trooper also appeared that year.

The 1981 also saw the agreement between GM, Isuzu, and Suzuki for the export of small cars to the USA, following which, in November 1984, Isuzu started supplying the American company with the Chevrolet Spectrum.

Isuzu's other international involvements are diesel engines for American Motors' jeeps (intended for the African and European markets), and gasoline and diesel engines to the Indian company Hindustan to go with Vauxhall (GM's English subsidiary) bodies. «Leyland Australia» Land Rovers also mount Isuzu engines. There are assembly plants in the Philippines, Thailand, Malaysia, Egypt and Tunisia. Production in the first half of the 1980s was based on the Spectrum (for the USA), Gemini, Florian/Aska (brought out in 1983 in a new version based on the General Motors «J-Car»), and Piazza/Impulse, as well as the off-road Trooper, the KB pick-up, and the small WFR (Fargo) van. The best year was 1981, with 129,564 cars built, while 1984 was down to 88,536. Exports account for 67.2% of production, with 41.7% going to the USA and 41.6% to Australia in 1984.

In the sphere of research and application of advanced technology, Isuzu has done significant work on adiabatic engines in collaboration with the Japanese chemicals giant Kyocera, and on electronics (most noteworthy being the automatic transmission system introduced on the Aska).

KB. The KB pick-up range includes rear-wheel drive and a number of 4-wheel drive versions. First brought out in 1971, it was offered with 1,584 and 1,949 cc gasoline engines and 1,951 and 2,238 cc diesel. Available alongside the basic model was one with a longer wheelbase, which was also offered as a «spacecab» (larger at the rear) or as a «crew-cab» with four doors.

Trooper/Rodeo Bighorn/Kangaroo. Launched in 1981, the Trooper is marketed in some places as Rodeo Bighorn, and in Australia (where it is assembled by Holden) as Kangaroo. Available as a convertible, with canvas or rigid roof, or as a station-wagon with either short or long wheelbase. Gasoline engines: 4-cylinder, 1,949 cc (88 hp) and 2,254 cc (110 hp). Diesel: 2,238 cc (61 hp suction, 75 hp turbocharged). Five-speed manual transmission and 2-speed transfer box. Four-wheel drive. Independent front suspension with wishbones and torsion bars; at the rear, rigid axle with semi-elliptic leafsprings.

Piazza/Impulse. Designed by Giorgio Giugiaro, the Piazza coupé came on to the market in 1981. Engines: 4-cylinder 1,949 cc either with one camshaft (120 hp), or two (130 hp); max. speed respectively 109 mph (175 km/h) and 112 mph (180 km/h), with Hitachi electronic injection; and 1,994 cc (180 hp) with turbocharger. For European markets a 102 hp version of the 1,949 cc engine. Five-speed transmission or 4-shift automatic; independent front suspension with wishbones; rigid rear axle.

Gemini. Brought out in 1974, the Gemini was due to the collaboration with General Motors. The body, chassis, and suspension were modelled directly on the European Opel Kadett, while the engines and fittings were developed by Isuzu. Included in the range was a coupé version. The engines were gasoline fueled, 1,584 cc (100 hp SAE) and 1,817 cc (110 hp SAE basic, 81 hp SAE for the United States «I-Mark» version, and 130 hp SAE in the sports version with two camshafts and electronic injection). According to the model, the gears were either 4- or 5-speed full-synchromesh, or 3-speed automatic. Certain stylistic modifications were made in 1979 (above, left). That year also a 4-cylinder 1,817 cc diesel engine was introduced (61 hp SAE at 5,000 rpm; 51 hp SAE for the USA) in both the sedan and the coupé. A 73 hp turbocharged version was then added in 1982.

In 1984 the Gemini range was totally changed, with the introduction of (among other things) front-wheel drive. Based on the General Motors «R-Car» design, this model comes either as a notchback four-door (above) or hatchback three-door sedan (left). The newly developed engines are 4-cylinder 1,297 cc (72 hp) and 1,471 cc (76 hp), plus a 1,487 cc diesel (52 hp). In the USA the Gemini FF is marketed as «I-Mark» or the Chevrolet Spectrum, and in Australia it is produced by Holden.

Florian/Aska. The Florian/Aska (1983) was Isuzu's first front-wheel drive car. Transverse engines: 4-cylinder 1,817 cc (93 or 105 hp), 1,994 cc (carburetor or injection, 110 and 115 hp respectively), 1,994 cc turbo (150 hp), diesel 1,995 cc suction (68 hp) and turbo (89 hp). Five speed manual gears. Standard McPherson front suspension; rigid axle, telescopic dampers and non-coaxial coil springs rear suspension.

WFR/Fargo. The Isuzu WFR or Fargo is a light commercial vehicle also available as a station-wagon (marketed too under the European Bedford trade mark as «Midi»). Four-cylinder engines: 1,995 and 2,189 cc diesel, and 1,817 cc gasoline.

Mazda

The Toyo Cork Kogyo was set up in Hiroshima in 1920. Having started as a cork factory, it expanded its activity two years later (after changing its corporate name to Toyo Kogyo Co.) to machine tools, then in 1930 to motorcycles. Their motorcycles enjoyed little success, and production ceased almost immediately. The year 1931 saw the first truck, the DA, with a 482 cc engine and load bearing capacity of 440.9 lbs (200 kg). Trading under the name Mazda, after the founder Jujiro Matsuda and the Zoroastrian god of light, Ahura Mazda, they built 66 vehicles in the first year of production.

The company's other area of diversification before the war was machine drills in 1935. However, there was already an active interest in automobiles, and this led to a prototype small sedan in 1940. Further development was then held up by the war.

Situated a little over 1.8 miles (3 km) from Hiroshima city center, Toyo Kogyo suffered relatively minor damage from the atomic bomb: broken windows and a blown off roof. Rebuilding began quickly, and production resumed in December 1945. After an experimental phase initiated in 1950, trucks began to come off the production line in 1958, and finally in 1960 the company's first car, the R-360, appeared (23,417 built in the first year). It was an attractive little coupé with an air-cooled 356 cc twin-cylinder V engine, developing 16 hp at 5,300 rpm, with a maximum speed of 56 mph (90 km/h). Powered by an almost identical engine, though water- rather than air-cooled, the P-360 Carol (either two- or four-door) appeared in 1962, capturing 67% of the home market for that category. Two other new models came out in 1964 and 1966 respectively, the 782 cc four-door Familia sedan, and the 1,500 cc Luce, a spacious car designed by the Italian designer Bertone.

Now the third biggest Japanese car manufacturer, Toyo Kogyo brought its production up to 54,000 in 1963, and over 81,000 in 1965.

In 1961 Mazda had acquired from NSU a license to build Wankel engines. However, without waiting for the first rotary engine to arrive from Germany, it produced its own

Familia. In 1964 first of the successful Familia range was the 800, a 782 cc 4-cylinder sedan (45 hp, max. speed 71 mph, 115 km/h). Engine: light alloy throughout, with side camshaft. Transmission: either 4-speed manual or 2-shift automatic with hydraulic converter. Shown here is the van version. Later there appeared the 985 cc coupé version with single overhead camshaft, producing 68 hp, and thus capable of a maximum speed of 90 mph (145 km/h). In 1970 the series was restyled, and the basic engine became the 1-liter, 4-cylinder model. Also available were a 1,272 cc (87 hp SAE) version, and a Wankel double rotary engine (491 cc x 2, 110 hp SAE) for the RX-100.

R-360. The first Mazda car was the little R-360 coupé (1960), with a rear V-2 air-cooled engine. As an alternative to the standard four-speed gears was an automatic gearbox with 2-speed converter. Max. speed 56 mph (90 km/h).

Carol. In 1962 appeared the 358 cc P-360 Carol (20 hp at 6,800 rpm), with a maximum speed of 65 mph (105 km/h). Two years later came the P-600 (586 cc, 28 hp).

Luce/Cosmo 929. The first Luce, with body designed by the Italian Bertone, came out in 1966 (left). A 4-cylinder 1,490 cc sedan (78 hp), it had a maximum speed of 93 mph (150 km/h). Next came the Wankel coupé (655 cc x 2), then in 1972 the second series, the 929, including a sedan and coupé (right) fitted (RX-4) with a Wankel engine (573 cc x 2) developing 120 hp SAE.

prototype. Three years later research in this area became centered in a new workshop with 30 test benches. The Mazda rotary engine came to differ more and more from its model, with substantial modifications resulting in better performance, fuel consumption, and reliability. The first result of all this research was the Cosmo 110S coupé, brought out in 1967. It had a 982 cc twin-rotor engine, the very first of its type to be mass produced on the world market, which developed almost 111 hp, giving a top speed of 115 mph (185 km/h). From then on Wankel engines became a normal feature of Mazda vehicles, in both production line and competition models: total sales of Wankel cars had reached 500,000 by 1973, and topped the million mark in 1978.

Exports to Europe and the United States began in 1966, with the Familia and Luce (the Asian market having been broached in 1961).

Of the overall 129,000 cars built in 1967, 16.4% were sold outside Japan, and this percentage rose in 1969 to 31% of a total of 201,133 Mazdas constructed. The range expanded with the Capella 616 series (1970), of which the Wankel version was called RX-2, the Grand Familia 808 or RX-3, and the Luce 929 or RX-4 (1972), and finally the Cosmo 121 or RX-5 (1975).

Mazda was hard hit by the crisis in the 1970s. Its middle-top range did not meet customers' new requirements, especially in the export market. In 1976 no production of any model exceeded 100,000, as against 715,000 Toyota Co-

Cosmo 110S. Presented as a prototype at the 1964 Tokyo Motor Show, the Cosmo 110S coupé began to be marketed in 1967. This was the first of the company's long series of Wankel powered cars. The original twin-rotor 491 cc x 2 model produced 111 hp with a maximum speed of 115 mph (185 km/h) already a significant advance on the 70 hp prototype. Subsequently the power was increased to 128 hp, and the speed reached 124 mph (200 km/h) in 1970. The production of this car was deleted in 1972.

Capella. The Capella range dates from 1970, when the 616 (left) was brought out (sedan and coupé versions, 4-cylinder, 1,490 and 1,586 cc, and on the «RX-2» a 573 cc x 2 Wankel). The Wankel developed 120 hp SAE. Appearing in 1979, in sedan (above) and hardtop models, the 626 had more powerful engines: 1,586, 1,769 and 1,970 cc (75 to 90 hp). The range received a general facelift in 1981.

Grand Familia. With the 1971 Grand Familia 808, the mid-size range became more luxurious. Available in sedan, coupé and station-wagon versions, it began life with 4-cylinder engines of 1,272 and 1,490 cc, and a Wankel (491 cc x 2) producing either 110 or 120 hp SAE (on the RX-3).

Chantez. In 1972 the range of small economy cars was renewed with the Chantez: 359 cc, water-cooled, two-stroke, 2 cylinders in line (35 hp SAE, with a max. speed of 71 mph, 115 km/h). Fully synchronized 4-speed gears.

rollas, 542,000 Nissan Sunnys, and 379,000 Honda Civics. With vast financial help from the Sumimoto Bank, Toyo Kogyo's biggest shareholder at the time, the company was able to develop a totally new mid-size Familia, the 323, which quickly restored its fortunes after the severe losses of the 1975 financial year. The new version of this car, brought out in 1980, was «Japanese Car of the Year.» Highly praised in the USA, Europe, and Australia, it sold 539,000 in 1981, representing 64% of Mazda's entire output. Barely 27 months after its appearance on the market, a million 323s had been built. At the same time there was an overhaul of the manufacturing process. The number of employees dropped from 36,000 in 1973 to 26,800 in 1978, with a considerable productivity increase: the turnover per head, for instance, soared from 12.9 million yen in 1973 to 40.8 million in 1981, and the number of cars per employee rose from 19 in 1975 to 43.7 in 1982. Quality control also improved considerably, and a «suggestions system» was introduced, with 59% of the 913,000 ideas suggested by the employees being adopted in 1980. The line saw a consistent evolution, with the Capella 626

Roadpacer. A large Wankel powered sedan (654 cc x 2), the Roadpacer came out in 1975. Producing 135 hp SAE, it featured traditional mechanical specifications, with rear-wheel drive and rigid rear axle. Despite its weight (empty) of 3,472 lb (1,575 kg) it was capable of up to 103 mph (165 km/h). Three-speed automatic gears, and drum brakes on all four wheels (optional front disc brakes).

Cosmo/Luce. Based mechanically on the Luce, the new Cosmo series appeared in 1975, consisting of a coupé entitled 121 in the fastback version (left) and 121L in the sedan version. Engines: 4-cylinder, 1,970 cc (87 hp) and Wankel 654 cc x 2 (for the RX-5) equivalent to 2,616 cc of a traditional engine. Partially restyled in 1979. The third generation Luce 929 sedan (right) came out in 1977 with 4-cylinder 1,769 and 1,970 cc engines and a Wankel 654 cc x 2 version. Five-speed manual transmission or 3-shift automatic. Some aesthetic changes were made in 1980. The 929 was also available as a station-wagon.

Pick-up. The little B 360 (above, left) and B 1500 (above) were the first Mazda pick-ups (brought out in 1961). Modified in 1965 and 1977 (left), this range was intended exclusively for export after the mid seventies, mostly to the United States, Canada and South Africa (1.6-, 1.8-, 2-, and 2.2-liter gasoline engines, and a 2.2-liter diesel). In 1985 a new series was launched, of which the example shown here (below) is the United States B 2000 version. Total production from 1961 to 1985 was almost 1.8 million.

Bongo/E Series. On the market since 1966, the Bongo or E Series transporter range offers vehicles that are useful both for commercial and passenger use. The engines range from 1.4- to 2-liter on the gasoline models, and include 2- and 2.2-liter diesel aspirated versions. Some models are four-wheel drive. It is marketed in some Asian countries as Ford J 80. Illustrated: the original Sky Lounge prototype.

Familia. In 1977 the Familia range was totally changed, with the launching of the two- or four-door sedan, station-wagon (above) and van 323, powered by 985, 1,272 and 1,416 cc 4-cylinder engines (45, 60 and 70 hp respectively). For some markets a Mitsubishi 1,597 cc (77 hp) engine was also available. The design was fairly conventional, with rear-wheel drive, McPherson front suspension, and rigid rear-axle; 4-speed synchronized gears (3-speed automatic gearbox available).

Savanna. Developed from the Grand Familia coupé, the more sporting RX-3 (or Savanna) appeared in 1971, with a 2-rotor 491 cc x 2 engine (110 hp, 4-speed synchronized gears, max. speed 109 mph, 175 km/h). The name Savanna was used again in 1978 for the new coupé RX-7 (Wankel 573 cc x 2) illustrated. This developed 130 hp SAE on the version intended for the home market, and for Europe and the United States 115 and 110 hp respectively. Four- or five-speed manual or 3-shift automatic transmission. In September 1983 the turbocharged version with electronic fuel injection came out (165 hp at 6,500 rpm), with a maximum speed of 137 mph (220 km/h). The RX-7 is much used for rallies and long-distance races. Over seven years (1978-1985) some 472,000 have been built.

Luce/Cosmo. In 1981 the 929, with the Luce models and the Cosmo sports series, was completely renewed, coming out in sedan, 4-door hardtop, and coupé versions. On the engineering side, the greatest innovation was the turbocharged version of the 12A rotary engine (573 cc x 2: equivalent to 2,292 cc), developing 165 hp. The other engines were: 4-cylinder 1,998 cc (110 hp), 2,209 cc (71 hp) diesel, and the Wankel 13B (2,616 cc, 160 hp). In the partial restyling of 1983, most changes were made on the coupé (above).

Familia. After a total updating in 1980, the 323 became the first front-wheel drive Mazda car. Independent suspension on all four wheels. Engines: 1,071 cc (55 hp), 1,296 cc (68 or 74 hp), and 1,490 cc (75, 85, or 88 hp). A 115 hp turbo version of the latter engine was introduced in 1983. Body types: hatchback with three (above left) or five doors (above right), sedan (below), and convertible. In Southeast Asia and Australia the Familia is marketed by Ford, the hatchback being called Laser, and the sedan, Meteor.

in 1979 after the 323, and the new Luce/Cosmo series in 1981. The Familia and Capella were then adapted to front-wheel drive in 1980 and 1982 respectively. The year 1978 saw the launching of the Wankel engine RX-7 sports car Savanna. Another factor in Toyo Kogyo's recovery was the acquisition of a roughly 24% shareholding by Ford in November 1979. This agreement benefited Mazda not only at the financial level but also commercially, as production could successfully be diversified with cars and small commercial vehicles selling in North America and throughout the Pacific area under the Ford trademark. This extra boost led to the new factory at Hofu, opened in 1982, and representing an investment of 35 billion yen. An ultra-modern complex capable of producing 20,000 complete cars and 7,000 CKD (Complete Knocked Down) units per month, it employs only 1,800 workers — and 155 robots. One vital feature of the plants is its flexibility, which makes it possible to produce individual models in small numbers profitably: nine different types of body can be pressed out, assembled, and painted, using three basic models.

Research has also developed considerably, the results showing in sophisticated prototypes such as the MX-02 (1983) and the 1985 MX-03 which, along with other innovations, features four-wheel steering system. Close collaboration with Ford, to whom Mazda supplies gasoline and diesel engines, has also led to an American production program at the new Flat Rock factory, aiming at 240,000 vehicles per annum by 1987. Mazda cars are also assembled in Australia, New Zealand, Malaysia, the Philippines and Taiwan. From May 1, 1984 the name of the company changed from Toyo Kogyo to Mazda Motor Co. Produc-

Capella. Totally renewed in 1982, the Capella became front-wheel drive and acquired new body designs. Four- or five-door sedan (above), and coupé (below) were available. The engines, now transverse, had capacities of 1,587, 1,789, and 1,998 cc (from 81 hp for the 1.6-liter version, to 145 hp for the 2-liter turbo). Completing the range is a 1,998 cc, 72 hp diesel engine model. Between September 1982 and August 1985 some 905,000 were produced. In 1983 the 626 was voted «Japanese Car of the Year» and (by the American magazine *Motor Trend*) «Import Car of the Year.» In certain parts of Asia it is marketed as Ford Telstar.

tion for the first half of the 1980s was between 736,000 and 862,000, with 73.5% exported in 1984. The United States market (in which in 1985 Mazda could boast 1.9% penetration) absorbs around 30% of all the cars exported by the Hiroshima company. Mazda is involved in long-distance races and produces Sport Prototypes with rotary engines, whose successes include a first place (in its class) in the 1983 24-Hour Le Mans race.

Familia. In 1985 sales of front-wheel drive Familia cars reached two million. That year the range was completely redesigned, with more roomy and aerodynamically built bodies (sedan, three- and five-door hatchback). Engines: 1,296 cc (74 hp) and 1,490 cc (86 hp, carburetor, 96 hp fuel injection, 116 hp turbo), both 4-cylinder. The more sporting model was supplied with a new 1,597 cc engine with four valves per cylinder and turbocharger (140 hp), and among other features has a three setting system for modulating the damping force of the rear shock absorbers. Completing the range is the 1,720 cc (59 hp) diesel model.

Mitsubishi

The Mitsubishi Motor Co. is part of the Mitsubishi Corporation, which employs approximately 10% of the total Japanese labor force, and which produces 12% of Japan's gross national product. Though modern car production only began in 1960, the origins of the group go much farther back, having a long history of involvement in the motor business.

This huge industrial empire started life as a small shipping company (Tsukuma-Shokai, founded in 1870 by Yataro Iwasaki). Gradually it increased and became more diversified, moving from shipbuilding to finance, to mining, to chemicals, to insurance. The name Mitsubishi featured first in 1875. In Japanese it means «three diamonds», and the company trademark now is three stylized diamonds. After World War I the chairman, Koyota Iwasaki, who had studied at Oxford, made Mitsubishi a holding company, having sectors with independent financial and management structures. During the first 30 years of the twentieth century these increased steadily in number. Vehicle manufacture began in 1917, when the Mitsubishi Shipbuilding Co. built the first series-produced Japanese car, the Model A (4-cylinder, 1,846 cc, 19 hp). Produc-

Model A. The first Mitsubishi automobile was brought out in 1917 and was the first Japanese car to be built in series by a big factory.

A10. Mitsubishi's first modern car was the small two-door 500 type A10 (twin-cylinder, four-stroke, 493 cc, 21 hp at 5,000 rpm), which was only a little over 9.84 ft (3 m) in length. It had independent suspension on all four wheels, and drum brakes. Three-speed gears, the two upper ones synchronized. Max. speed 56 mph (90 km/h).

Minica. The Minica 360 (1962) represented a new departure in the small car range. Available as either a sedan (left) or station-wagon, it had a 359 cc two-stroke twin-cylinder engine, air-cooled, developing 18 hp, with a maximum speed of 55 mph (89 km/h). Four-speed transmission; independent front suspension, rear rigid axle with semi-elliptic leafsprings. A new version available as sedan, van, and Skipper coupé (right) came out in 1969. The 30 hp engine was air-cooled, the 38 hp version water-cooled. Also, coil springs rather than leafsprings at the rear.

Colt 1500/1200. In 1966 there came out a larger sedan, at first with a 1,498 cc, 70 hp engine (Colt 1500, above), then with a new 1,189 cc, 62 hp version (Colt 1200), giving a max. speed of 81 mph (130 km/h). Two-door and station-wagon models were also available. Three-shift automatic transmission available as an alternative to the standard 4-speed synchronized manual gearbox.

Mitsubishi again turned to cars, bringing out the A10 500 in 1960, a small economy car with rear air-cooled engine, which sold until 1963.

In 1962 there appeared the Minica and the Colt (359 and 594 cc respectively), with continual technical and design modifications as the mainstay of production throughout the 1960s. The year 1964 saw the launch of the luxurious Debonair sedan. Production rose steadily: from 5,203 in 1960 (including a mere 11 exports), to 15,882 in 1963, then

Colt 600/800/1000. In 1962 the 2-cylinder 594 cc (25 hp) Colt 600 (top) appeared, representing a first venture into a category higher than the small Minica. This development was pursued the following year, with the launch of the four-door Colt 1000 sedan (center) (4-cylinder, 977 cc), and in 1965 with the original three-door fastback (above) Colt 800 (3-cylinder, 843 cc, 45 hp). The 1-liter engine was then fitted also on the fastback in 1966, when a new 4-cylinder 1,088 cc four-door version was brought out.

Colt Galant/Lancer. In the early 1970s the mid-size range sedan was extended with the Colt Galant (1970, above) and Colt Lancer (1973, below). The former (also available as a station-wagon) had 1,439 and 1,597 cc engines, and there was a 1,686 cc coupé version as well. In Lancer range available as two- or four-door sedan, the engines were 1,189, 1,439 and 1,597 cc.

tion continued, though not on a large scale, until 1921, the company having decided to concentrate exclusively on industrial vehicles. The first of these came on the market in 1918. From 1920 they were built under the trademark FUSO. In 1934 the Mitsubishi Shipbuilding Co. merged with the Mitsubishi Aircraft Co. to form the Mitsubishi Heavy Industries Co., which the following year launched the first Japanese diesel truck.

Production during World War II centered mainly on airplanes, with above all the outstanding Zero fighter plane. Production resumed almost immediately after hostilities ceased, the first widely distributed vehicle being the Silver Pigeon motorscooter (1946), which played a significant part in the motorization of Japan. There then followed the small Mizushima truck. For two years from 1953 Mitsubishi managed the importation of Kaiser-Frazer jeeps, in the form of CKD (Complete Knocked Down) units. The American company then ceased trading. After a complete overhaul of the diesel truck and bus sectors,

45,905 in 1965 and 105,952 in 1967, with very modest export quotas.

At the international level, after the first foreign factory was opened in Thailand in 1965, exports to the USA began in 1970. That same year the company finally became the Mitsubishi Motor Corporation, and negotiations opened for the acquisition by Chrysler of a 15% shareholding (this being successfully concluded in 1971). From 1969 to 1970 car production rose from 127,812 to 246,422. Another leap forward occurred in 1978, after a static period due to the oil crisis, with the launch of the new Galant and Colt. So successful were these both at home and abroad that production that year rocketed to over 400,000, and increased of 28.3% over the previous year.

Important advances were also made in the racing field, with a Colt winning the Australian «Southern Cross Ral-

Minica. A further Minica series appeared in 1972: the F4 (above) had the same displacement, and all models were water-cooled. Later came the Ami 55 (546 cc, 31 hp, 68-75 mph), with the same bodywork.

Galant Sigma. In 1976 came the Galant Sigma (above, left), which was then lightly restyled in 1980 (above). Available also as a station-wagon or coupé (left), it had 1,597, 1,796, and 1,997 cc (also supercharged) engines, plus a 2,555 cc 135 hp model for the faster coupé. In the USA the sedan was sold as the Dodge Challenger and the coupé as the Plymouth Sapporo.

Lancer/Celeste. The Lancer range was renewed in 1976 (right). Traditional in concept, with rear-wheel drive and rigid rear axle, the new series had a variety of engines: 1,244 cc (55 hp), 1,410 cc (68 or 80 hp), 1,597 cc (78, 84, or 86 hp), 1,796 cc turbo (135 hp) and 1,995 cc (105 hp; 170 supercharged). Preceding this sedan was the Celeste coupé (below), launched in 1975, with the same general design and the same engines. For the US market (where it sold as Plymouth Arrow) a 4-cylinder, 2,555 cc engine was fitted, producing 106 hp at 5,000 rpm. On both the sedan and coupé the gears were 4- or 5-speed, according to the version, or 3-shift automatic. Developed directly from the Colt (of which it was the notchback version), the new front-wheel drive Lancer series came out in 1982 (below, right). Henceforward production included equally both front- and rear- (EX) wheel drive models.

Pajero. Selling on other markets as Montero or Shogun, the Pajero first came out in 1981. Available as a three- or five-door station-wagon (right), canvas-top and metal-top (left), with four-wheel drive, it has 1,997 cc (available a turbocharged version) and 2,555 cc gasoline engines, and a 2,346 cc diesel with or without turbocharger. Between 75 and 120 hp. Five-speed manual transmission with high-low transfer box. Rear limited slip differential. Mitsubishi also produces a Jeep version (canvas top or station-wagon) under license. Engines: 1,995 and 2,555 cc gasoline, and 2,659 cc diesel (all Japanese made). Four-speed gears with high-low transfer box. Rigid axle suspension: both front and rear.

Colt/Mirage. Presented in prototype at the 1977 Tokyo Motor Show, the new Colt (Mirage for the Japanese market) started selling the following year. Mitsubishi's first front-wheel drive model with transverse engine, it offered displacement of 1,244 cc (72 hp), 1,410 cc (82 hp; 105 hp turbo), and 1,597 cc (85 hp). In the USA it was marketed under the name Dodge Colt or Plymouth Champ (64 hp and 72 hp SAE). One of the more interesting innovations on this model was the new transmission system: a second lever allows to select a low or high ratio for each of the standard four speed.

ly» in 1967 and 1968, then a Galant in 1971 and 1972. Then in 1973 a Lancer came overall first in the same rally, going on to win the «East African Safari Rally» the following year.

Mitsubishi enjoyed a particularly good year in 1978: an output of 628,886 cars made it the third largest Japanese manufacturer (while in the first half of the 1980s it dropped to fifth, or fourth if truck production is also taken into account, with 591,980 cars built in 1984). Mitsubishi accounted for 8.1% of Japanese car exports in 1984, with 378,337 foreign sales, of which 35.9% were to North America, 29% to Europe, and 14.7% to Australia.

Interests abroad are based in 33 assembly factories (15 in Asia, 9 in Africa) and in commercial enterprises in North America. In the United States Chrysler distributes the Colt and the Starion under its own trademark, while the Mitsubishi Motor Sales of America, founded in 1981, handles the company's other models directly. In 1982 the first foreign test center was opened, at Ann Arbor in Michigan, for developing and testing vehicles for the American market. Small-car production on United States soil is object of a joint-venture with Chrysler and it is forecasted to begin operation in 1988. An important European agreement is that with Daimler-Benz, for the development in common of a commercial vehicle to be produced from 1987 in the German company's Spanish factories.

In Australia Mitsubishi has total control of the local

Tredia/Cordia. The Tredia sedan (below) and Cordia coupé range came out in October 1981. Mechanically identical, they have front-wheel drive and 4-cylinder transverse engines, 1,411, 1,597 and 1,795 cc (the latter developing 90 or 100 hp or 135 hp turbo). The 1.8 liter 100 hp Tredia and the 1.8 liter turbo Cordia are also available with four-wheel drive (above Cordia). Transmission: Super Shift, with power and economy program giving a total of eight-speed. A 3-speed automatic gearbox model is available on request, while the supercharged versions have 5-speed transmission.

Starion. Launched in 1982, the sports coupé Starion has a 4-cylinder 1,997 cc supercharged engine (145, 180, or 200 hp). Marketed in the United States under the name Dodge Conquest, it is supplied there with a 4-cylinder 2,555 cc supercharged engine (145 hp). Rear-wheel drive with five-speed transmission. Body design offers a good coefficient of penetration: $Cd = 0.35$.

Chrysler branch, as well as assembling some of its own models. From the point of view of technology important results have been obtained, such as the sophisticated DASH (Dual Action Super Head) electronic system of secondary intake valve control, introduced in the 2-liter Sirius engine, and the ECS (Electronic Controlled Suspension). Specially significant was the acquisition by Porsche of the silent shafts (a balancer shaft) developed by Mitsubishi for its own 4-cylinders. Porsche has incorporated silent shaft in the engine of its new 944. Also worth recalling is the use of ceramics for some engine parts (rocker arm) and the introduction on the mass market for the first time in 1982 of liquid crystal display instrument panel in the Cordia model.

Mitsubishi's involvement in racing has been primarily in the sphere of rallying: worthy of note here would be the third place (overall) in the 1982 Finnish «Thousand Lakes» won by a Lancer Turbo, and the first place (overall) achieved by the off-road Pajero in the 1985 «Paris-Dakar Rally.»

Minica/Econo. Front-wheel drive was first introduced in Minica or Econo series in 1984. The transverse 546 cc twin-cylinder engine now produced 31 hp (basic version) and 39 hp (turbo), with speed of 68 and 71 mph (110 and 115 km/h) respectively. Overhead camshaft and three valves per cylinder. Four-speed transmission and drum brakes.

Chariot/Space Wagon/Colt Vista. The Chariot (sold in Europe as Space Wagon and in the USA as Colt Vista) came out in 1983. It is a large car with 1,597 and 1,795 cc (available also in turbocharged version) engines, plus a 1,997 cc model, fitted on the four-wheel drive version brought out in 1984. Alternatives to the 2-liter model's 5-speed gearbox are 4-speed gears with transfer box, or 3-speed automatic.

Colt/Mirage/Lancer. The Colt (Mirage), and Lancer series was totally changed in September 1983. The former hatchback has three (above) or five doors (above, right), while the latter (selling on the home market as Lancer Fiore) is a classic notchback sedan with four doors (right) also available as a station-wagon. Engines: 1,198 cc (40 hp), 1,299 cc (77 hp), 1,468 cc (87 hp), and 1,598 cc supercharged (120 hp; for the USA 102 hp). There is also a 65 hp diesel engine. In the United States they are marketed by Chrysler as Dodge Colt and Plymouth Colt. Transmission: 4-speed (also with supplementary «economy» program) or 5-speed manual, or 3-speed automatic. The old rear-wheel drive Lancer series is still supplied alongside the more up-to-date 1983 version (engines: 1.4- to 1.8-liter, 80 to 160 hp).

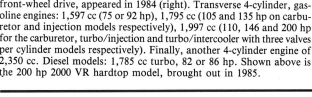

Galant. A new Galant series, redesigned throughout and modified to front-wheel drive, appeared in 1984 (right). Transverse 4-cylinder, gasoline engines: 1,597 cc (75 or 92 hp), 1,795 cc (105 and 135 hp on carburetor and injection models respectively), 1,997 cc (110, 146 and 200 hp for the carburetor, turbo/injection and turbo/intercooler with three valves per cylinder models respectively). Finally, another 4-cylinder engine of 2,350 cc. Diesel models: 1,785 cc turbo, 82 or 86 hp. Shown above is the 200 hp 2000 VR hardtop model, brought out in 1985.

Delica. On February 1985, Delica 4WD, one of the Mitsubishi light commercial vehicles, was honored as «4-wheel drive of the year» in the Australian magazine *Overlander*.

Nissan

The Nissan Motor Co. dates back to 1911, when Masujiro Hashimoto founded in Tokyo the Kwaishinsha Co. whose first car, the DAT, came out in 1914. Tradition has it that the name DAT (the Japanese for «hare») was derived from the initials of the surnames of Kenjiro Den (who had helped Hashimoto set up the company), Rokuro Aoyama, a childhood friend, and Meitaro Takeuchi, a cousin of the former prime minister Yoshida, who had hel-

DAT 41. Begun by Kwaishinsha in 1916, production of the DAT 41 continued under the new company DAT Jidosha Seizo Co. It was a 4-cylinder 15,8 hp sedan (above). Below, the DAT 51 Torpedo (1923).

ped subsidize the venture. The DAT was produced on a regular commercial scale, although in limited numbers. In 1919 another company, the Jitsuyo Jidosha Co. in Osaka, launched the small 1,260 cc Lila. In 1925 the Kwaishinsha Co. and the Jitsuyo Jidosha merged to form the DAT Jidosha Seizo Co. Based in Osaka, the new firm continued production of the Lila and DAT 41 (a small 4-cylinder water-cooled model), but then turned exclusively to industrial vehicles. Meanwhile the corporate name changed, first to DAT Motor Car Co., and then to DAT Automobile Manufacturing Co. A new car, the DAT 91, appeared in 1930. The following year, during which the company was absorbed into the Tobata Imono Co., another small car was launched, called the «Datson» («son of DAT» as per the English meaning). In Japanese, however, this word sounded too like the word for «ruin,» and since a new Jidosha factory had been destroyed by a hurricane, at about that time the name was altered to «Datsun,» as a sort of invocation to the sun for protection against further disasters. The first Datsun, the Type 10, thus appeared in 1932. On December 26 the next year, the Tobata and the Nihon Sangyo Co. formed the Jidosha Seizo Co. (based in Yokohama, with a capital of 10 million yen) for car production. In 1934 this company finally took Nissan Motor Co. as its corporate name.

The early Datsuns were used almost exclusively as taxis, while exports of CKD units, which began that same year (1934) rose to substantial figures after 1940. Production in the Yokohama factory had become fully integrated by 1935. In 1936, when the Datsun 15 was launched, an agreement for technical cooperation was concluded with Graham-Paige in America, who were just then bringing out the 2.8 liter 6-cylinder economy car Crusader. The Crusader formed the model for the Japanese company's new series inaugurated in 1937 under the Nissan trademark a name that was to become associated with the most luxurious models. The first of this series to come out was the 70 (6-cylinder, 85 hp), available in either sedan or phaeton.

Racing had meanwhile become more popular in Japan, and the 1936 Japan Motor Vehicle Competition run on the Tamagawa circuit was won by a small single-seater 747 cc Datsun.

Production of Datsun cars ceased in 1938, in favor of industrial vehicles. During World War II Nissan was fully involved in the Japanese war effort, setting up an aircraft engine factory at Yoshiwara in 1943. Under the US occupation after the war, in 1947, this factory recommenced production, with prewar Datsun and Nissan models. Of particular importance to the company was the agree-

Lila. In 1919 Jitsuyo Jidosha brought out the Lila, a small car with a 1,260 cc 8.5 hp engine. Illustrated two models: the four-seater JC (1924) sedan (left) and the roadster version (right).

ment concluded in 1952 for production under license of Austin cars.

The first Anglo-Japanese car (the A40) appeared that same year, and was followed in 1955 by the A50. English engineering influence grew, leading to a series of 4-cylinder 850 cc side valve engines which were incorporated in the new Datsuns launched in 1955 and subsequently. In 1956 even the Austins built under license started to be made with all Japanese parts. The years 1953 and 1954 had been difficult for Nissan: a long run of strikes brought the company to the verge of bankruptcy. Rescue came from the Industrial Bank of Japan, which still remains the biggest shareholder (6.01% in 1985). Once the things got back to normal the All Nissan Motor Workers' Union was created, establishing a close and profitable collaboration between workers and management.

In 1954 US control ended. Acquisition of Western technology was vital since, with the Nissan name less highly considered than rivals such as Toyota, it helped the com-

pany gain a reputation for mechanical excellence, making up for the financial problems. Racing also helped here, Datsun coming into the international limelight for the first time when a 210 (Fuji-Go) came first in its class in the 1958 Australian Rally. Also in 1958 for the first time, small Japanese cars were shown in the Los Angeles Imported Car Show, after which a commercial network was set up in the United States. Based in Los Angeles and New York, this soon spread over virtually the whole country.

In 1959 the Datsun 310 was produced (4-cylinder, 1,189 cc), the first of the lucky Bluebird series. Nissan's performance during the 1950s (throughout which it kept ahead of all the other Japanese car manufacturers) can best be shown in figures: in 1950 car production totalled a bare 865; by 1955 this had risen to more than 7,800; the following year it leapt to twice that, topping 20,000 in 1957, exceeding 32,000 in 1959, and reaching about 66,000 by 1960 (when approximately 4,750 complete cars were exported). The next decade began with a process of internationaliza-

Type 10. The first car produced under the Datsun name was the Type 10 in 1932 (4-cylinder, 747 cc), of which we here see the sedan version.

Type 70. A new series of more prestigious cars was launched in 1937, under the name Nissan. First of the series was the 70 (6-cylinder, 85 hp), built in joint-venture with the American company Graham-Paige.

Type 14, 15, 16. With minor mechanical and design modifications, Datsuns models continued to be produced until the outbreak of World War II. Top a 14 torpedo, which came out in 1934. Below: a 15; it had the same body of the 14 and was launched in 1936. Bottom: the Type 16 sedan introduced in 1937.

210. In the 1958 «210» (above) the displacement of the 4-cylinder Datsun was raised to 988 cc (37 hp). That same year a 210 Fuji-Go came first of Class A in the Round Australia Mobile Gas Trial.

Type 110. Production of the Austin A40 under license, begun in 1952, enabled Nissan to acquire the English company's valuable know-how, on which were based the successive Datsun models such as the 1955 Type 110, with four-cylinder, 850 cc.

Type DS. In the early postwar years Datsun developed a series of models based on cars produced before the war. From left to right: the DS (1949), DS-2 Thrift (1951), and Thrift DS-4 (1952), all sedan models.

Above, the Sakura which finished fourth in the Round Australia Mobile Gas Trial.

310, 410 DX. The 310 (1959) launched the Bluebird series. This (above) is the DX version (4-cylinder, 1,189 cc; 3-speed gearbox). Front suspension: wishbones coil springs and hydraulic dampers; rear suspension: rigid axle, leafsprings.
In 1963 the new 410 model appeared (below), completely redesigned with a 1,299 cc 67 hp SAE engine 87 mph (140 km/h). Three-speed gearbox or fully synchronized 4-gear or automatic 3-speed. Integral chassis.

tion, importation and distribution companies being set up in the USA (Nissan Motor Co. based in Los Angeles) in 1960, Canada in 1964, and Australia in 1966. Five years after the foundation of the Nissan Mexicana SA de CV in 1961, this became the company's first foreign assembly plant, followed in 1967 by others in Peru. In Japan factories were built at Oppama and Zama in 1962 and 1965 respectively, while in 1966 the Prince Motor Co. was taken over, its Gloria and Skyline models remaining in production.

The Nissan brand name was readopted in 1960 for the company's top models. The Cedric appeared (with 1.8- to 2-liter engines), followed by the President (in 1965), the first luxury car to be built in Japan. In 1966 a Nissan Prince Royal became the first Japanese car to be used by the imperial family.

Throughout the 1960s Nissan production continued to rise steadily, although in 1965 Toyota stepped into the lead

S211 Sport. The company's first sports car, the start of the Fairlady series, was this S211 Sport (1959), replaced in 1962 by the almost identical SP213 (4-cylinder, 1,189 cc, 60 hp SAE at 5,000 rpm, 4-speed gearbox, first gear not synchronized and maximum speed 81 mph, 130 km/h).

Sunny. First of the Sunny series was the B10 in 1965, which came in two versions, sedan or station-wagon. The engine was 4-cylinder in line, 988 cc (62 hp SAE at 6,000 rpm). Fully synchronized 3- or 4-speed gears. Maximum speed: 84 mph (135 km/h) for the sedan, 81 mph (130 km/h) for the station-wagon. Left, the 1000 DX (1966).

Skyline. In 1957 Prince launched the Skyline (left), a 4-cylinder 1,484 cc sedan, 73 hp SAE at 4,800 rpm. A later alternative was a 6-cylinder, 1,862 cc engine, developing 83 hp SAE at 4,800 rpm. Right, the new 1963 model produced for a short time under the Nissan trademark after the take over of Prince in 1966.

Cedric. The Cedric range dated back to 1960, when a 4-cylinder sedan (1,883 cc, 83 hp at 4,800 rpm) was launched (top). Totally redesigned in 1965. A luxury series is the Cedric Special 6 (above), with 6-cylinder engine, 1,973 cc (110 hp SAE at 5,200 rpm) and 3- or 4-speed gearbox. Maximum speed 93 mph (150 km/h).

President. In 1965, with the President (top) Nissan entered the world of prestige cars. Available engines: 6-cylinder in line (2,974 cc, 130 hp SAE), or V8 (3,988 cc, 180 hp SAE). New bodywork was designed in 1973 (above), while the displacement of the 8-cylinder engine raised to 4,414 cc (200 hp).

Fairlady/Silvia. Datsun sports models kept the name Fairlady, and the coupés the name Silvia throughout the 1960s. Above, the 1962 and 1965 models. With 4-cylinder engines, 1,595 cc, 90 hp at 6,000 rpm, these cars had a maximum speed of 106 and 103 mph (170 and 165 km/h) respectively, with acceleration from 0 to 62 mph (100 km/h) in 11.0 and 12.7 seconds. Four-speed gears; front disc brakes. In 1969 the sports Fairlady Z came out (below), the first of a long series of successful coupés. It was available in two versions, both with 6-cylinder engines (1,998 cc), either 130 hp SAE, or a more powerful 160 hp SAE (the Z 432).

Laurel. Launched in 1968, the Laurel range came in sedan or hardtop models with 4-cylinder engines, 1,815 or 1,990 cc, developing between 105 and 125 hp. Independent suspension on all four wheels. The 2000 GL illustrated here (110 hp at 5,600 rpm) had either a 4- or 5-speed mechanical gearbox, or an automatic with three speeds.

Skyline. In 1968 the Skyline range was totally redesigned, the new models being a four-door sedan and a two-door hardtop. The engines available were from 4 cylinders of 1,483 cc (95 hp) or 1,815 cc (105 hp) to 6 cylinders of 1,998 cc (120 hp at 6,000 rpm, rising to 160 at 7,000 rpm in the three carburetor GT-R illustrated here, with a maximum speed of 124 mph, 200 km/h).

Cherry. The company's first front-wheel drive car was the Cherry (left), brought out in 1970. Available as four-door sedan or two-door coupé they had 4-cylinder engines, either 988 cc (58 hp) or 1,171 cc (80 hp). Front disc brakes; 3- or 4-speed transmission. In 1978 the range was fully renewed, being sold in certain markets (including the United States) under the name Pulsar. The engines offered were 988, 1,270, or 1,487 cc, and the bodywork, hatchback (above), coupé, and station-wagon.

Sunny. A new version of the Sunny appeared in 1970 (sedan and coupé), either 1,171 cc (68 or 83 hp) or 1,428 cc (85 or 95 hp). Above, left Sunny Excellent 1400 GL. Another complete change of design came in 1973, of which this (above right) is the four-door sedan model. In 1977 the model was restyled once again: (below right) the 1.5-liter sedan and (below, left) the 210 coupé intended for the US market. The coupé 210, which had a 4-cylinder (1,397 cc) engine, came third (after two diesel fueled Volkswagens) in a competition sponsored by the US Environmental Protection Agency to check consumption, covering an average of 29,6 miles on a gallon of gasoline.

among Japanese car manufacturers. Production figures grew from 91,000 in 1961 to 213,000 in 1964, 572,000 in 1968 and around 950,000 in 1970. An increasingly high proportion went for export: 7.2% in 1960, 11% in 1962, 24.7% in 1966, and 34.2% in 1970. In 1967 a wharf at the port of Hommoku was created exclusively for Nissan export vehicles.

At the technical level, meanwhile, Datsun and Nissan cars were proving equal to Western vehicles. Examples might include the 1967 Bluebird, with integral chassis and fully synchronized gears and the 1970 Cherry, the company's first front-wheel drive car. During the 1970s the basic models were the Cherry/Pulsar (1,000-1,400 cc); Laurel (1,800-2,000 cc); Skyline (1,600-2,000 cc); Cedric and Gloria (2,000-2,600 cc); President (3,000-4,400 cc), and the sports Fairlady/240 Z, launched in 1969. In 1969 the first multiple-arm robot was introduced in the Oppama factory, forerunner of the 1,600 similar machines at work in Nissan's Japanese plants in 1985.

In the racing sphere too during this period there were notable achievements: in 1967 the prototype R-380 broke a number of world records, while two years later the Japanese Grand Prix was won by the R-382, a large 6-liter sports car (600 hp, 186 mph, 350 km/h). In 1970 a Datsun 1600 won the East African Safari, and this success was repeated in 1972 with a 240Z. The latter model came fifth and third in the Monte Carlo Rally in 1971 and 1972 respectively.

Further important contracts were agreed in the 1970s, with Mazda and Ford, thus creating the Japan Automatic Transmission Co. Ltd. (1970), now with all Japanese capital, and then the Japan Electronic Control System Co. (1973) with Bosch. Hitachi later replaced the German firm in collaboration on electronic systems for cars. Meanwhile the numbers of cars coming off the assembly lines increased gradually, to over 1,751,000 in 1978, with 835,000 going to markets abroad, representing 28% of Japanese car exports overall.

By the first half of the 1980s Nissan remained a steady second in the Japanese car industry line-up, with production leveling at around 1,850,000 (i.e. 26% of national production), of which in 1984 some 1,012,000 went for export. To the export figures an approximate 175,000 CKD sets should also be added. Total exports of CKD units since the first auspicious beginnings with the Yue Loong Motor Co. of Taiwan in 1959, up to 1984, amount to 3.7 million.

Bluebird. The Bluebird 510, launched in 1967, was updated with inno-vations like integral chassis, fully synchronized gears and alternator. Avai-lable engines: 1.3-liter (72 hp SAE) and 1.5 liter (100 hp SAE), both 4-cylinder. In 1971 came the new 610 model (right: the hardtop version). For this a 1.8-liter engine was designed; then in 1973 a 2-liter (125 hp) engine was mounted on the GTX. The range was then redesigned in 1976 (810/180 series), with 1,595, 1,770 and 1,998 cc engines. Above: the 180B sedan de Luxe; above right: the 1800 SSS-ES version.

Skyline. With 1.6-, 1.8- and 2.0-liter engines, the Skyline range was to-tally restyled in 1972, and the C110 series introduced, followed by the C210 in 1977. Above: the 1972 GT-R, 6-cylinder, 1,998 cc, 160 hp. Right: the 1977 240K hardtop version, with the same engine, but 130 hp.

Violet/Stanza/Auster. The Violet was first produced in 1973 (above), with 1.4- or 1.6- liter engines. In 1977 came a new series, sold also un-der the names Stanza and Auster. Right: the 1800 GTE coupé (1977). In both 1979 and 1980 a Violet sedan won the African Safari Rally. Above right: the 160J sedan (1980).

Silvia/Gazelle. The name Silvia, dropped in 1968, reappeared in 1975 with the S10 (above), a 1.8- or 2.0- liter coupé. In 1979 the range was totally renewed, selling also under the name Gazelle. The most powerful model was the 1800 LSE-X (right), 4-cylinder, 1,770 cc with turbocharger, 135 hp at 6,000 rpm. 5-speed transmission, disc brakes on all four wheels. Maximum speed 112 mph (180 km/h).

Gloria/Cedric. Also marketed under the name Gloria, the Cedric is a top-size sedan, totally renewed in 1971, 1975 (above), 1979 (above, right), and 1983 (right). On the last version the engines mounted were either 4-cylinder (1,973 cc) or V6 (2,960 cc, 148 hp at 4,800 rpm). Maximum speed: 109 and 118 mph (175 and 190 km/h) respectively.

Laurel. Development of the Laurel line continued with the new series of 1977 (above: the sedan) and 1980 (above right), offering a vast choice of engines: 4-cylinder (1,770 cc, 105 hp; or 1,952 cc, 110 hp); 6-cylinder, 1,998 cc (carburetor, injection, and turbo versions), 145 hp; 6-cylinder, 2,393 and 2,753 cc, or diesel 1,952 and 2,792 cc. In 1984 the bodywork was radically restyled (right) and a new 4-cylinder turbo engine supplied (1,998 cc, 145 hp).

Fairlady. The new Fairlady Z series was presented in 1978: two or four-seat versions, both with original T-bar roof. The basic model had a 6-cylinder engine, 1,998 cc, 125 hp at 6,000 rpm, while the 280 Z (above) had 2,753 cc (also 6 cylinders) developing 148 hp at 5,250 rpm. Heading the range, the 280 ZX Turbo (below), with the same 2.8-liter engine, plus Garrett turbocharger, developed 200 hp at 5,200 rpm. All versions had 5-speed gearbox or 3-speed automatic.

Major international agreements have also been reached recently.

In 1980 Nissan acquired 35% of the Spanish Motor Iberica from Massey Ferguson, and this involvement has rise steadily, to 84.4% at the present time. In January 1983 the first off-road Patrol, marketed under the trade-mark Ebro, drove out of the gates of the Barcelona factory, which in 1984 built over 6,000 for the EEC market.

In June 1983 production of the Arna (based on the Nissan Pulsar) began in the Italian factory at Pratola Serra, the fruit of a joint-venture between Nissan and Alfa Romeo. Some 31,000 of these cars were built in 1984. An agreement was reached with Volkswagen in 1981 for production of the Volkswagen Santana in Nissan's Zama factory — which got under way in December 1983. August 1984 saw the first shipment of Pulsar series cars to the Australian company General Motors-Holden, for whom a new engine had been designed (6 cylinders in line).

In the United States Nissan began production of commercial vehicles (10,000 per month) at its plant in Smyrna, Tennessee in June 1983; then in March 1985 the production of the Sentra, based on the Sunny. The Smyrna factory is one of the most up-to-date in the world, completely computer controlled, with 228 robots. By 1987 it will be able to produce 240,000 vehicles per annum.

In 1983, the company's 50th anniversary year, work also started at the Mexican factory at Aguascalientes, for the construction of 110,000 Sunny engines per year, to be added to the cars assembled at Cuervanaca with components made at Lerma.

February 1984 brought an agreement with the British government (Britain is Nissan's second largest export customer, taking 112,000 vehicles in 1984) for production of the Stanza at the new factory at Washington, in the northeast of England. India too has become a major Nissan market, after the contract negotiated with the government in November 1984 for the supply of 1.2 liter engines to the Premier, to be mounted in the bodywork of the old Fiat 124 as from August 1985. Future collaboration will also include export of CKD units.

Bluebird. Yet another new Bluebird series appeared in 1979 (above: the hardtop version). In 1981 a 1,952 cc diesel engine was introduced, developing 65 hp at 4,600 rpm. Another new model in 1983, with 1.6-, 1.8-, and 2.0-liter, 4-cylinder engines, and 2.0-liter, V6-cylinder on the Maxima. The SSS-E illustrated below has a 1.8-liter suction (97 hp) or turbo (134 hp) engine.

Skyline. In 1981 a new version of the Skyline came out (below the coupé). The range of engines designed for this line were one 4-cylinder (1,990 cc) and two V6-cylinder (2,393 and 2,753 cc), plus 2.0- and 2.8-liter diesels. Top of the range was a supercharged version: the 2.0-liter RS (above) engine, 4 valves per cylinder, with turbocharger and intercooler, developing 205 hp at 6,400 rpm.

Sunny/Sentra. The three-door hatchback, four-door sedan and coupé versions of the 1981 Sunny range. Produced in the United States under the name Sentra, these models had 4-cylinder engines, 1,270 and 1,488 cc (gasoline) and 1,681 cc (diesel), from 61 hp (the gasoline version) to 116 (the 1.5 liter turbo). Five-speed standard transmission on all versions, automatic on request. Power-steering as optional extra. Some versions are marketed as Laurel Spirit.

Pulsar/Cherry/Langley/Liberta Villa. Included in the Pulsar range, introduced in 1982, are a notchback sedan (left), a hatchback sedan (right) and a coupé (below). For some markets and some models the names Cherry, Langley, or Liberta Villa are used. The basic model has a 4-cylinder engine (987 cc, 50 hp); also available is a 1,270 cc (60 hp) or 1,488 cc (75 hp) standard or 115 hp with turbocharger and electronic fuel injection. The coupé with this engine goes up to 112 mph (180 km/h). The hatchback version is also produced in Italy, incorporating the 4-cylinder Alfa Romeo boxer (1,186 or 1,351 cc) and marketed under the name Alfa Romeo Arna, or for certain markets Nissan Cherry Europe.

Leopard. Launched in 1980, the Leopard (left) series has the following engines: 4-cylinder (1,770 cc, 105 hp), 6-cylinder in line (1,998 cc, 125 hp in the suction version, 145 in the turbo), a turbocharged V6 (2,960 cc, 230 hp at 5,200 rpm). Above: the turbo hardtop.

Stanza. Updated in 1981, the Stanza (or Auster, Violet, or Liberta) range offers a hatchback and notchback sedan. Engines: 4-cylinder, 1,598 cc (90 hp) or 1809 cc (101 or 110 hp).

Overall, Nissan production outside Japan, which in 1975 represented 9% of its total (188,000), had reached 10.8% in 1978, and 16.5% in 1984, while in 1985 it was up to 18.8%, a total of more than 550,000 vehicles.

Exports (these figures are those for 1984) went mostly to North America (47.3% of the total, of which 93% to the United States), then to Western Europe (24.3%), the Middle East (10.3%), Southeast Asia (7%), Latin America and the Caribbean (3.5%), Australasia (4%) and Africa (3.3%).

On the technical side, the major developments over the last decade, during which the company has evolved its own distinctive philosophy, have been in the areas of energy-saving, safety, electronics, and use of new materials, in the search for ever lower consumption (resulting in the 1982 NRV-II prototype), the main aim has been to reduce the weight of the vehicle through extensive use of plastics, as in the windows and windscreen for instance (a weight-saving of 30%).

Positive safety improvements have been researched in depth, resulting in electronic systems that indicate the correct stopping distance and help keep the driver alert by means of sensor controls on the steering wheel and other devices such as indicators of mileage covered and atmospheric conditions, together with visual and aural suggestions that it is time for a halt. This system, called «Safety Drive Adviser» was incorporated in the Bluebird in October 1983.

Electronics began to make an appearance in normal production with the ECCS system (Electronic Concentrated Engine Control System), in 1979, which maintains fuel injection, ignition timing, exhaust gas recirculation, the idle speed and air/fuel ratio at optimum levels under all driving conditions. In May 1983 the Cedric, Fairlady Z, and Laurel were equipped with an automatic wiper system, that senses rain drops and adjusts its intermittent action to rain intensity. Worth noting too is the electronically controlled, three-way power-steering introduced on the 1983 Blue-

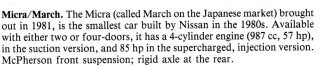

Micra/March. The Micra (called March on the Japanese market) brought out in 1981, is the smallest car built by Nissan in the 1980s. Available with either two or four-doors, it has a 4-cylinder engine (987 cc, 57 hp), in the suction version, and 85 hp in the supercharged, injection version. McPherson front suspension; rigid axle at the rear.

Prairie/Stanza Wagon/Multi. In 1982 Nissan produced its first space-wagon, the Prairie, marketed in the United States as Stanza Wagon and in Canada as Multi. With 1.5- and 1.8-liter engines (between 75 and 110 hp), the main features are its height (5.24 ft, 1.6 m) with sliding rear doors.

159

Fairlady. In September 1983 the new Fairlady Z range appeared. The 300 ZX coupé has two supercharged V6 engines, 2,960 cc, 160 or 200 hp (aspirated or turbocharged versions); with maximum speed for the latter of 137 mph (220 km/h). Two or four seater models

Silvia/Gazelle. The Silvia (or Gazelle) coupé appeared in a new series in 1983. There were two basic engines, both 4-cylinder, 1,809 and 1,990 cc, 100 and 150 hp respectively. The turbocharged versions were also available (135 and 190 hp; the maximum speed of the latter 134 mph, 215 km/h). The 2.0-liter engine features four valves per cylinder and an electronic fuel injection system.

bird, which automatically reduced the level of power assistance for steering as the speed of the car increases. The driver can also select three different levels of assistance. In October 1984 the Bluebird Maxima appeared with «Supersonic Suspension System», which automatically selected the best damper setting from soft, medium, or firm by means of five sensors. The system automatically selects firmer damping at speeds of more than 50 mph (80 km/h).

The development of new materials resulted in, among other things, ceramic elements in the turbocharger and composites for certain parts of the suspension.

Shown at Tokyo in 1985, the CUE-X prototype demonstrates everything the most advanced technology in the area of car manufacture can produce. A luxury sedan with numerous innovations in engine, bodywork, and suspension, it boasts a coefficient of penetration (Cd) of 0.24 and an electronically controlled retractable rear spoiler. Research and development of new technology are undertaken by Nissan both in Japan, in five plants specializing in different areas, and abroad — the Nissan Design International Center at San Diego, California, and the sophisticated laboratories at Ann Arbor, Michigan. There is also an European design center in Brussels.

Pick-up. Nissan production includes a vaste range of commercial vehicles equipped with gasoline and diesel engines. In 1980 the company added new four-wheel drive versions, available in the Long Body (two-seater) and in the Double Cab (four- or five-seater).

Today Nissan is a giant enterprise with 14 factories in Japan and 24 assembly plants in 21 countries. The mother company, Nissan Motor Co., has an annual turnover in excess of 3.5 billion yen (1985-1986 financial year). To this can be added the gross turnover of all the controlled companies, including Nissan Diesel and the Fuji Heavy Industries, which own the Subaru brand name.
Nissan's interests are not confined to motor vehicles: other sectors include textile machinery, aerospace, elevator cars, industrial engines, shipping and marine engines.

Patrol/Safari. The off-road Patrol/Safari, a 6-cylinder engine with power ranging from 95 to 120 hp on the diesel version and 134 hp on the gasoline model. Illustrated is the station-wagon model.

URVA-Vanette. The last generation of Nissan's microbuses: on the left the URVA Bus Transporter; on the right the Vanette Bus Transporter.

Subaru

«Subaru» is the trade name used by the car sector of «Fuji Heavy Industries Ltd,» a group with interests in various different industries (aircraft, railways, agriculture, ship-building and bus bodywork and container, as well as cars and light commercial vehicles).

A relatively young company, it dates back to 1917, when the Nakajiama aeronautical research laboratory was founded. This developed successfully for some 30 years, undergoing a total reorganization in 1945, with the creation of «Fuji Sangyo Ltd.» Production was then diversified, entering the motorscooter, bus bodywork, and rolling stock sectors. It also produced a range of gasoline engines. After the war the occupying forces split the group into twelve independent companies, six of which were then reunited to form «Fuji Heavy Industries» in July 1953. «Subaru», the name chosen for this group's cars, is a Japanese reference to the Pleiades of Greek mythology, the six stars which are in the Taurus constellation, intended as symbols of the companies of which the new enterprise was made up.

The first car, the 360, appeared in 1958. A typical early Japanese economy car, it was a small sedan with rear-mounted two-stroke twin-cylinder engine. In the first year 604 were produced. Production rose steeply, to 5,111 in 1959 and 22,319 two years later.

In 1966 the FF-1 was introduced. This front-wheel drive, middle range sedan carried a 977 cc engine, 4-cylinder boxer a design to which Subaru always remained faithful.

FF-1. The front-wheel drive FF-1 (4-cylinder 977 cc boxer engine) appeared in 1966. 55 hp at 6,000 rpm, max. speed 81 mph (130 km/h). Later, the displacement raised to 1,088 cc (62 hp; 90 mph, 145 km/h), and in 1970 a 1,267 cc (80 hp, 99 mph,160 km/h) version, the 1300 G, came out. The FF-1 came either as a two- or four-door sedan, or two- or four-door station-wagon.

With the agreement for collaboration with Nissan in 1960, Fuji production rose over the subsequent decade, topping 100,000 for the first time in 1968 (exports that year representing 73.2 per cent). Sales to Europe began in 1965. The early seventies saw an extensive updating of Subaru cars: in the small economy car range the 360 was replaced by the front-wheel drive R-2 in 1970, then the Rex in 1972, while in October 1971 the FF-1 was superseded by the new Leone, which was to become the company's best selling car (only two years later more than 100,000 were made, out of an overall approx. 130,000 and 30,000 of these went to the United States). The oil crisis affected the numbers of Subaru cars produced in 1974 and 1975, but in 1976 the previous records were broken, with annual production rising to some 150,000 in 1979 and exceeding 202,000 in 1980. Exports, which in 1975 represented 26.9% of production, reached 46.5% in 1979.

Unlike other Japanese car manufacturers, Fuji had no foreign involvements in the car sector, in the way of assembly plants abroad or joint venture agreements with Western companies. All its interests were concentrated in factories at home, at Gunma, Yajima, Kirin, Mitaka, and Oizumi. (However, there were assembly plants for small commercial vehicles in Taiwan, New Zealand, and Spain). The Leone's success on the international market was due

360. Subaru entered the car market in 1958 with the 360. Available also as a sports car, it was barely 9.8 ft (2.99 m) long, with a rear-mounted two-stroke twin-cylinder engine (356 cc, 16 hp at 4,500 rpm, later increased to 20 hp at 5,000 rpm). Air-cooled. A 422 cc (22 hp) version was also brought out, called Maia or K212; 3-speed gears and four-wheel independent suspension.

R-2. The company's initial 360 was totally redesigned in 1970, and marketed under the name R-2. Of the early model only the structure and the displacement of the engine remained (32 hp at 6,500 rpm basic, and 36 hp at 7,000 rpm on the SS). Fully synchronized 4-speed gearbox. Maximum speed between 71 mph (115 km/h) and 75 mph (120 km/h) according to the model.

in no small degree to its four-wheel drive system, introduced in 1974. This was the company's most distinctive production feature at least until the first half of the eighties, when all the major car producers followed suit in incorporating four-wheel drive on normal cars not built specifically for rough driving. At all events, Subaru can rightly claim to have pioneered this now popular technology. 4 × 4 cars represent 40% of the Fuji turnover (672.1 bil-

Leone. The pride of the Subaru range is the Leone, which first appeared in 1971 as a sedan (below), station-wagon, and coupé (above). It had front-wheel drive. The four-wheel independent suspension incorporated a torsion bar system on the rear. Engines: the FF-1's 1,088, and a similarly conceived 1,361 cc boxer (either 80 or 93 hp). Fully synchronized 4-speed gearbox, and front disc brakes (standard on the more powerful models, fitted by request on the slower ones).

Rex. The 1972 Rex (above) was mechanically the same as the R-2, but had a more modern four-seat body. The first engine was the familiar 356 cc (though with a water-cooling system). In October 1973 a four-stroke twin-cylinder engine was introduced (358 cc, 28 hp at 7,500 rpm), then in 1976 there appeared the 490 cc Rex 5 (31 hp at 6,200 rpm), and the following year the 544 cc Rex 550 (the same power, but with considerably improved torque).

Rex. A new Rex series (above) came out in August 1981, 10.5 ft (3.2 m) long, with either three or five doors. The basic engine was the twin-cylinder 544 cc (Rex 550), which in 1984 also became available with turbo (41 hp at 6,000 rpm). The Rex 700 was 665 cc, 37 hp. In 1986 a four-wheel drive model became available.

lion yen in the 1985 financial year). After 15 years of steady growth, production had risen to 242,680 (in 1985), of which 53% were exported (these figures include the Pulsar's assembled for Nissan). The main importers of Subaru cars are the USA (58.1% of exports), West Germany (6.4%), and Switzerland (5.3%).
In the 1980s the three basic models have been the Rex (totally redesigned in 1983) and Justy in the small car range, and the Leone in the middle range. Along with these goes the XT (Alcyone) sports model, brought out in 1985. Among the technical innovations on the most recent models are: automatic four-wheel drive according to road conditions, and the «Hill Holder» braking system, which prevents the car rolling backward on steep slopes.

Leone. The Leone range was completely renewed in 1979 re-appearing in sedan (above), station-wagon (right), hardtop (below), and hatchback (below right) versions. On all these versions there featured four-wheel drive optional. Engines: four horizontally opposed cylinders, 1,298 cc (61 or 72 hp), 1,595 cc (71 or 87 hp), or 1,781 cc (80 or 100 hp). The models intended for the United States had 1.6- and 1.8-liter engines (68 and 73 hp SAE respectively). In 1983 the 1,781 cc model also became available with turbocharger (120 hp).

Justy. With the Justy in 1984 Subaru entered the 1-liter class. A compact hatchback sedan, it had a 3-cylinder engine (997 cc, 55 hp at 6,000 rpm). Also available with four-wheel drive, it came with either 4-speed manual gears or automatic transmission.

Leone. October 1984 saw the launch of the third generation Leone, with a new sedan (left) and station-wagon body (right) design, still available as either front-wheel drive or «4WD». The supercharged 1.8-liter with electronic injection increased in power to 135 hp at 5,600 rpm. On the four-wheel drive models there was also a 2-speed transfer box.

XT/Alcyone. Brought out in 1985, the XT (Alcyone) coupé, mounting a 1.8-liter turbo engine, was also available as either front-wheel drive or four-wheel drive. With a particularly good penetration factor (Cd = 0.29), this two-seater sports model shares the same dual automatic levelling control as the Leone turbo. On both versions the gears are either 5-speed or automatic.

Rex Combi, E 10. Completing this survey of Subaru production, here are two series of light commercial vehicles: the Rex Combi (left), developed from the small 2-cylinder car; and the E 10 (right), developed from the Justy. Both are also available with four-wheel drive.

Suzuki

Suzuki, the third biggest Japanese motorcycle manufacturer, only began making cars in 1956, but the company in fact dates back to the first decade of this century, when in 1909 Michio Suzuki founded the Suzuki Loom Works at Hamamatsu, for the production of textile machinery. It was not until 1952, however, that Suzuki produced its first vehicle, a small motorcycle (two-stroke, 36 cc), the Power Free. This was really a motorized bicycle. Nevertheless, it was the first of a series that was to achieve considerable success, both commercially and in sports, throughout the world. In 1954 the company changed its name to Suzuki Motor Co. October 1955 saw their first four-wheeler, a 360 cc car with a two-stroke twin-cylinder en-gine, called the Suzulight. Over the next two years, how-ever, only 43 of these were built. Car manufacturing be-gan in significant quantity in 1962, when the company pro-duced 2,565 Suzulight 360 TLs, with a 21 hp SAE engine and a maximum speed of 53 mph (85 km/h).

In 1964 the Fronte appeared, with a 3-cylinder, 785 cc en-gine, then three years later, a 360 version which replaced the old Suzulight. Production rose substantially between 1967 and 1970, during which period the new factories at Iwata, Toyama, Osuka and Kosai were opened.

The company's interests were not confined to cars and other kinds of private and commercial motorvehicles: it also produced outboard motors and prefabricated hou-

Fronte 800. In 1964 the 3-cylinder, two-stroke Fronte sedan came out (785 cc, 41 hp at 4,000 rpm). Front-wheel drive with four fully synchro-nized gears. Integral chassis, fully independent suspension, with drum brakes both front and back. Max. speed 75 mph (120 km/h).

Suzulight. Suzuki's first venture into car manufacture was the Suzulight (above), a small front-wheel drive vehicle with an air-cooled two-stroke twin-cylinder engine (360 cc). Only 43 were made. Regular production only really began with the Suzulight 360 (below) in 1962, mounting a similar engine (21 hp, max. speed 53 mph, 85 km/h, 4-speed gears, first not synchronized). It had a backbone chassis and four-wheel indepen-dent suspension with transverse leafsprings on both axles.

Fronte 360. In 1967 the Suzulight was replaced by the more up-to-date Fronte 360 or LC 10 with a compact, lightweight rear engine (air-cooled, 3-cylinder, two-stroke: 25 hp at 5,000 rpm basic, and 36 hp at 7,000 rpm in the SS version). It had three carburetors, and was guaranteed a long life by a camshaft with 7 crankshaft bearings. Fully independent suspen-sion. Max. speed 58 mph (110 km/h) for the less powerful model, and 78 mph (125 km/h) for the SS.

Fronte/Alto/Cervo. The range of small Suzuki cars was renewed in 1970 with the Fronte LC 50 (above left), which though the same mechanically, had a totally new body. The 3-cylinder 360 cc engine (31 to 36 hp according to the model) was transverse cantilever on the rear axle. In 1976 a new 443 cc series appeared, to be followed the next year by the 539 cc Cervo coupé (above right). Brought out in 1979, the front-wheel drive Fronte /Alto (below left) represented a technical revolution, with a four-stroke 543 cc transverse engine offered as an alternative to the two-stroke 539 cc model. Also supplied with a 4-cylinder 970 cc engine for certain markets, the Cervo was then totally redesigned in 1982, similarly adopting front-wheel drive. The following year brought (below, right) the Cervo De Tomaso Turbo (543 cc supercharged, 40 hp at 6,000 rpm). Based on the Cervo coupé is the Mighty Boy pick-up.

Alto/Fronte. Based on the 1982 Cervo coupé, the new Alto/Fronte series appeared on the international market in 1984 (543 and 796 cc, 31 and 40 hp respectively, 3 cylinders). Penetration coefficient (Cd) of 0.36. Rotating driver's seat for easier access. The Alto also comes with four-wheel drive.

167

ses. Its cars (121,871 produced in 1969) were still based on the Fronte, which was updated in 1970, then again in 1976 and 1979. A coupé version, the Cervo, came out in 1977, with a 3-cylinder 539 cc engine, or (for export) 4-cylinder 970 cc. An original series of small, off-road four-wheel drive cars (Jimny) was launched in 1970. First of the series was the LJ-10, with two-stroke twin-cylinder engine, 359 cc, 25 hp at 5,000 rpm. On asphalt the maximum speed was 47 mph (75 km/h). There then followed the LJ-55 (539 cc) and LJ-80 (797 cc). Exports were modest: an approximate 5.5% of a total of 69,798 vehicles built in 1979. This figure was considerably higher the next year — 23,249 vehicles, representing 24.6% of total production.

In August 1981 Suzuki entered into an important deal with General Motors for the sale of small economy cars in the United States. At this point the giant American business acquired an approximate 5% shareholding in Suzuki, and a further 3.5% with its Japanese partner Isuzu.

In collaboration together, the two Japanese companies then produced a new 1,000 cc car, sold in Japan as Suzuki Cultus and in the United States (after April 1984) as Chevrolet Sprint. In this same year exports from the Hamamatsu company thus benefited greatly, rising to 101,865 (56.8% of total production of 179,311 cars).

Important European contracts were also made: in the spring of 1984 Land-Rover Santana SA in Madrid purchased the license to build Suzuki's Jimny LJ-410 in Spain, at the rate of about 10,000 per year. Other Suzuki assembly plants exist in Canada, China, India and Pakistan. Suzuki cars in the first half of the eighties are variants on three basic models: the Fronte (Alto)/Cervo, the Cultus/Swift, and the Jimny. In 1985 two interesting sports prototypes were brought out: the R/P2 (800 cc supercharged with intercooler 12 valves and four-wheel drive) and the R/S1 (1,300 cc central engine, with 16 valves).

Cultus/Swift. Launched in 1983, the three- or five-door Suzuki Cultus (or Swift on certain markets) marketed in the United States as Chevrolet Sprint or Pontiac Firefly. Front-wheel drive. Engines: 3 cylinders 993 cc, 50 hp (or in the USA 48 hp) or 80 hp turbo and 4 cylinders 1,324 cc (66 or 72 hp basic or GS respectively). Optional 5-speed mechanical gearbox or 3-shift automatic. McPherson front suspension, rigid rear axle.

Jimny. After its first appearance in 1970 (above), the off-road Jimny steadily evolved. From the original twin-cylinder two-stroke LJ-10 (359 cc) were developed the LJ-55 and LJ-80 (539 and 797 cc), and then in 1980 the new SJ series. This consists of the SJ-30 (3 cylinders, two-stroke, 539 cc), SJ-410 (4 cylinders, four-stroke, 970 cc) and SJ-413 (brought out in 1984: 1,324 cc, 63 hp). The four-wheel drive is disengageable on the front wheels, and the 5-speed transmission have a transfer box acting on each gear. Different bodies are mounted on the same ladder frame chassis: canvas top (above right), long-body (right), metal top (below left) and pick-up (below right).

Every/Carry. Suzuki also produces a series of small commercial vehicles. This was then replaced by the Every/Carry series (ST30 and ST40). Engines: 3 cylinders 993 cc; and for certain markets 4 cylinders 970 cc. Some versions come with four-wheel drive. Left, Carry Space Kombi bus; above, Super Carry high-roof van TX.

Toyota

It seemed folly to many to attempt to create an all-Japanese car factory, starting from nothing, at a time when the American giants, General Motors and Ford, who were decades ahead in terms of production and marketing techniques, seemed on the point of establishing their own assembly plants on Japanese soil. However, this in no way discouraged Kiichiro Toyoda, the eldest son of Sakichi Toyoda who in 1926, with only his own energy and inventive genius behind him, built up a flourishing modern textile machine business, the Toyoda Automatic Loom Works Ltd. In 1933, with a capital of £ 100,000 (raised on the sale of some patents for automatic looms to an English firm), Kiichiro set up a new section in his father's company, for the manufacture of cars. Japanese technological know-how in the automobile world was still very restricted, and the first prototype, the A-1 (1935), of which

only three were produced, was closely similar to the Chrysler Airflow, one of the most sophisticated American cars of the time. On August 1937 the Koromo factory was completed, representing an overall investment of 12 million yen (originally a small farming town, Koromo is now nicknamed the «Toyota City»). The newly founded Toyota Motor Co.'s first car, the AA, was developed directly from the first prototype: a 6-cylinder, 3.4-liter sedan, capable of 62 hp. In the first month only 150 were built, but Kiichiro's faith in the future of Japanese cars led him to invest another 45 million yen in a new factory at Honsha in 1938, and to improve the total capacity of his plant. The company's corporate name was Toyota rather than Toyoda in order to stress the social value of the new business, rather than its family background.

New materials and technology had to be developed to com-

A-1. The first Toyota prototype, the A-1, appeared in 1935. Modeled on the American Chrysler Airflow, it had a 6-cylinder engine (3.4-liter, 62 hp). Only three were built.

AA, AB, AC. Directly derived from the earlier prototype, the AA (1936) was the first mass produced model. It came in a sedan version (above) and a phaeton version (AB, above, right): 1,404 of the former were built, production ceasing in 1943, while the latter remained in production until 1942, with 353 being sold in all. In 1943, under the new name AC (right), the power was raised to 75 hp; 115 of these cars were produced. Maximum speed 62 mph (100 km/h).

AE, BA, B. A smaller and stylistically more original model, the AE (above, left), came out in 1939, with a 4-cylinder, 2,258 cc, 48 hp engine. It remained in production until 1943. Brought out in 1940, the BA (above), with the same engine, was styled on the Volvo PV60. Production began three years later. In 1944 the B sedan (left) mounted an «old» 6-cylinder engine (3.4-liter, 85 hp). Maximum speed 75 mph (120 km/h). This prototype never entered regular production.

pensate for the lack of natural resources in Japan, so consequently over the next few years a company was started to investigate the possibilities of electric motors, and a research center was built. A further two companies for steelworks and machine tools and auto parts were created in 1940 and 1941. Also in 1940 appeared the new BA: entering production in 1943, this car abandoned American models, taking its inspiration from the PV60 a model produced in Europe by the Swedish Volvo.

During the Pacific War only industrial vehicles could be built, and even then there were many problems. Car production was interrupted in 1944. Trucks came off the assembly lines without radiator grilles, with parts of the bodywork and seats made out of wood, brakes on the rear wheels only, and a single front headlight: usable parts from wrecked or worn-out trucks going to make up «recycled»

SA, SC, SD, SF. Toyota's first postwar car, launched in 1947, was the SA (above). With a 4-cylinder engine (995 cc, 27 hp), it had a maximum speed of 54 mph (87 km/h). In production until 1952, only 215 were sold. However, it was the first of a long series of models with the same engine: SC, SD (right, top), and SF (right). The SF alone was produced in any sizeable quantity (3,653), between 1951 and 1953 (these sales were due to increased demand for taxis in this period).

vehicles. Under the occupation after the war, Toyota was allowed to resume regular production of trucks almost immediately. But permission to recommence car production was not granted until 1949. In the meantime, however, the technological foundations of the future automobile industry had been laid, with research concentrating on small cars that would not compete directly with the large American models. The first prototype of the new S series was completed in January 1947, with technical innovations

RH. With similar body to the SF, but with a more powerful 4-cylinder engine (1,453 cc, 48 hp), the RH Super was brought out in 1953, and remained in production until 1955. In all 5,845 were made, and it was eventually replaced by the Crown RS.

such as (for the first time in Japan) a backbone chassis and coil springs suspension.

Yet car production did not resume under favorable auspices. Financial difficulties forced Toyota to accept long delays in payment from its commercial outlets, who needed to place a sufficient number of cars on the market; this led to liquidity problems which, with a lack of adequate backing, made it even difficult for the company to pay its salaries regularly. The management proposed to reduce production, but this set off a long series of strikes which merely worsened the company's debt, bringing it to the verge of bankruptcy.

Radical changes were made, one of which was the creation of a new company to market Toyota production both at home and abroad. This, the Toyota Motor Sales Co., began business in 1950. Meanwhile long negotiations with the workers had led to agreement on a reduction of the workforce from 8,000 to 6,000. Thus the strike, (the only one in the whole history of the company) ended, and a relationship was established between management and workers in which each side acknowledged that each was vital to their common interests.

Kiichiro, the company's founder, the real pioneer of Japanese motoring, died in 1952.

During the fifties massive investments went in to renovating plant. One novelty introduced at this time was the «suggestion system,» whereby workers were encouraged to make constructive suggestions as to how production might be improved (the idea came from Ford, which the Toyota top management visited and studied closely in 1950). As an indication of the success of this system, we

Crown. The first Crown models (left) were launched in 1955, with the same engine as the earlier RH, and were the first Toyota series to be exported to the United States (August 1957). In 1958 a Crown unexpectedly came third in the Round Australia Rally. In 1960 a new 1,879 cc engine was fitted, then in 1962 the model was totally changed (above), and a more modern X frame adopted. At first only available with a 4-cylinder, 1.9-liter (90 hp) engine, from 1965 it was also supplied with a 6-cylinder, 1,988 cc engine. There was also a station-wagon version. By 1963 14% of Crowns had automatic gears.

Publica/1000/Starlet. Plans for a small economy car were begun in 1954 and led finally to the Publica (above), brought out in 1961 for the home market, with a twin-cylinder 697 cc (28 hp) air-cooled engine. The 1000 export model had a 1-liter engine. Between 1962 and 1964, a station-wagon, convertible, and pick-up came out in the same range. Dating from 1965, the Sport 800 (below) had a 2-cylinder engine (790 cc, developing 45 hp SAE) with a maximum speed of 96 mph (155 km/h). An updated version of the Publica appeared in 1966 (right), modified at front and rear, and mounting a 790 cc engine.

Corona. Production of the Corona series started in 1957, and by 1984 over 5.6 million were made. By the mid 1960s it had become established as Toyota's major success on the international markets. Brought out in May 1957, the first generation, the ST10 (above, left), had a 4-cylinder, 995 cc, 33 hp engine. This was replaced two years later by the 997 cc PT10. Sales increased substantially with the introduction of an updated version (PT20) in 1960, with production that year touching 25,000. A new 1,453 cc (60 hp) engine was introduced in 1961. Above, the 1961 RT20. The third generation Corona, brought out in 1964, had integral chassis and a 1.5-liter (70 hp) engine, and immediately became a best-seller on the Japanese market. As well as the four-door sedan (below, left), there was a station-wagon, a two-door hardtop (below, right the 1970 Mark II 1900), and a five-door sedan. In 1969 the Corona was judged «Imported Car of the Year» by the American magazine *Road Test*.

need only look at the figures: of a thousand suggestions considered in 1951, 23% were adopted; by 1960 the number of suggestions had soared to 5,000 (33% adopted); 385,000 in 1975 (83% taken up); and 1,906,000 in 1982 (95% adopted). Car production rose from 1,857 in 1950 to 12,000 in 1956 (partly helped by the demand for taxis at the time). At the end of the decade Toyota's annual production capacity exceeded 30,000.

Unlike other Japanese manufacturers, Toyota chose not to make Western cars under license, concentrating rather on developing its own original models. On the one hand this gave the company a better defined image than its competitors, but on the other it meant that huge resources had to be channeled into research and development. The range of vehicles meanwhile increased rapidly: from the off-road BJ (1951), re-named Land Cruiser three years later, to the Crown (1955), the first authentically all-Japanese car. At the same time there was a wide range of diesel trucks. In 1957 the little Corona was launched, and an important commercial experiment began with the

first exports of the Crown to the United States, where the ground had been prepared by the setting up of the Toyota Motor Sales USA Inc. (1957). This venture was a complete failure: the cars were quite unsuited to long distance driving at sustained speed (driving patterns in Japan at the time were exactly the opposite).

From this negative experience, however, Toyota learnt some lessons. A six-year technology development program was initiated, which in the end came up with a result tailored specifically for the American market.

Continuous improvement in Japan's economic situation during the sixties had a beneficial effect on home sales of the more popular cars such as the Toyota Publica (1961) and, in particular, the new Corolla (launched in November 1966), which immediately became the number 1 Japanese economy car.

Car production reached 129,000 in 1963, topped 230,000 in 1965, and from 659,000 in 1968 reached 964,000 in 1969. Exports steadily grew too, from a bare 1,810 in 1960 to over 17,700 in 1964, and from about 111,500 in 1967 to almost 287,400 in 1969. By the end of the decade Toyota exports accounted for 46% of all the cars exported from Japan; on the USA market it rose to 53.4%, and Toyota sales there were second only to Volkswagen among all car importers. Export of CKD units also led to the creation of assembly plants, usually with exclusively local capital, in South Africa (1962), Australia (1963), Thailand (1964), Peru (1967), and Portugal and Malaysia (1968).

At home meanwhile the company continued to expand more aggressively, taking over control of two other car manufacturers, Hino in 1966, and Daihatsu in 1967.

More stringent controls on investments had been introduced by the Japanese government in 1971, leading other manufacturers to negotiate cooperative contracts with foreign companies, especially the American «Big Three,» but Toyota held out on its own, setting itself ambitious targets for more business and lower production costs. Two years later, with the first oil crisis (1973), strategy was substantially changed, but Toyota never abandoned its confidence in cars as indispensable agents of individual freedom. And despite the risks in holding onto such an attitude, an aggressive expansion policy was developed. At the same time it was realized that more flexible production systems had to be introduced to meet the ever more varied demands of different markets. A shrewd salary po-

licy and a remarkable «company spirit» both helped Toyota through this difficult period.

To keep production costs down, everything was worked out down to the final detail — even ways of saving on office air-conditioning, and using both sides of business document papers. The production cycle itself was rationalised: in the pressing shed, for instance, the ends of spools of steel which had previously been thrown away, were now kept, saving 2.5 tons of steel a month. Such economies did not, however, stand in the way of new production of technically more sophisticated cars (e.g. the Sprinter, Carina, and Celica).

New factories were opened in the seventies (Tsutsumi, Myochi, Shimoyama, Kinu-ura, Tahara), bringing car production up from over a million in 1970, to around 1,632,000 in 1973, to 1,715,000 in 1975 and to over two million in 1978. Car exports continued to increase (32.4% in 1970, 35.7% in 1975, 42.9% in 1979). CKD unit exports in 1979 reached 150,000, some of which went to new establishments in Pakistan, Trinidad, Indonesia, Kenya. Technically, Toyota cars evolved rapidly. Alongside advanced prototypes experimenting with new technology for the future, electronics came to play a bigger part in normal mass produced models. Back in 1968, for instance, an automatic cruising speed regulator had been introduced

2000 GT. The prototype 2000 GT was brought out in 1965, but had no great commercial success. A sporting coupé, it had a 6-cylinder, 1,988 cc engine (150 hp at 6,600 rpm). A 200 hp competition model was also made.

Crown. Designed with the American market in mind, the third generation Crown, brought out in 1967, had a new chassis to meet America's strict new regulations on passive safety standards. It was also at last more powerful and more comfortable over long journeys. Engine: 2-liter, 105 hp. For the Japanese market there was also a new 4-cylinder, 1,994 cc engine. Along with a station-wagon version, a hardtop (above) was also introduced in 1968. The fourth generation (below) came out in 1971, with better aerodynamic design and attractive technical innovations such as an electronic anti-skid (ESC) system on the brakes, and electronically controlled automatic transmission (EAT). The existing 2-liter models were complemented with a 6-cylinder, 2,563 cc engine.

Publica/1000. Powered by twin-cylinder (790 cc, 40 hp SAE) and 4-cylinder (933 and 1,166 cc, 58 and 68 hp SAE respectively) engines, the third version of the 1000 came out in 1969 and remained in production until 1978, when it was replaced by the Starlet range. Over 18 years some 1,350,000 Publica's were built.

Corona. With the same bodywork version as the previous version, the fourth generation Corona appeared in 1970. A new engine (1,707 cc, 95 or 105 hp SAE according to the desired compression ratio) was made available. For the hardtop there was also the option of a 1,858 cc engine (later, 1,968 cc, 120 hp SAE). Once again the Corona won good publicity in an American journal, when *Road and Track* voted it car of the year in 1971.

Corona Mk II/Cressida. The need to offer a superior model, particularly on the American market, led to the 1968 Corona Mk II or Cressida (four-door sedan, two-door hardtop, and station-wagon versions), initially a slightly elongated version of the Corona. The first series, of which the sedan (left) and hardtop (above, left) are shown here, had 4-cylinder engines, ranging from 1.5 to 1.9 liters. More individual styling and engineering were introduced on the Cressida Mk II in 1972, with the launching of the second generation (above, right), mounting 4-cylinder, 1.7 (later, 1.8) and 2.0-liter engines, or 6-cylinder engines, 1,988 and 2,253 cc. Some versions had electronic injection.

Corolla, Sprinter. After the first model launched in 1966, in 1970 the Corolla was brought out in a new series (left), at first with a 1,166 cc engine (68 or 77 hp SAE), then later in the same year with a 1,407 cc (86 hp SAE) engine. This was raised in 1973 to 1,588 cc, 102 hp SAE. The choice of models was: two- or four-door sedan, coupé and station-wagon. The most powerful coupé, the Corolla Levin, was a successful racing model, winning various races (in its category) including the 1975 Thousand Lakes Rally. With identical body design to the sedan and coupé Corolla, the new Sprinter series (right) also appeared in 1968, mounting the same engines as the models they were based on.

Corona. In 1973 came the fifth «generation» of Coronas, with 1.6- and 2.0-liter engines. Various safety devices began to be built-in developed from ESV experiments, and aimed also at increasing comfort. On the more de luxe models, for instance, there was a check-control. In 1977 overall production of the Corona reached 4 million (35% approximately exported).

Starlet. The Starlet, brought out with the 1000 in the economy range, appeared as a coupé (above) in 1973, with 993 and 1,166 cc engines. That same year the range was completed with a four-door model. A second line (below) came out in 1978, with newly styled three- or five-door body, and new 1,290 cc engine (72 hp): these models were more comfortable and more fuel efficient, and produced less pollution.

Crown. In 1974 the Crown was totally restyled (top) and the choice of engines widened with the introduction of a 2-liter, 6-cylinder engine with electronic injection (EFI), 135 hp SAE. In October 1977 there also came out a 4-cylinder (2,188 cc) diesel engine, making this the first diesel powered Toyota to be mass produced. In April 1979 the 2 millionth Crown came off the assembly line. That year also saw the sixth «generation» (above), in which the 2,563 cc engine was raised to 2,798 cc and supplied with electronic injection. Top range Toyota cars already featured check-controls and display monitors as standard. With all the various different engines and styles of body (four-door, two- or four-door hardtop, station-wagon) there was a selection of 70 different versions.

on the de luxe Century, then gradually extended to the cheaper ranges. In 1971 the Mark II incorporated an electronic injection control system (EFI), which was then used into all the company's gasoline cars. Also in 1971 the first Toyota Crown came on the market with an ESC (Electronic Skid Control) system on the brakes — another feature now adopted on a whole range of Toyota cars.

Appearing in 1978, the small Tercel Sedan, Toyota's first front-wheel drive car, once and for all closed the technological gap between Japan and the West.

The 1970s will in part be remembered for the anti-pollution policies implemented by certain countries in the sphere of automobile production, and for the ever greater need to cut fuel consumption.

Following the December 1970 «Muskie Act» issued by the American Congress, and the similar laws introduced in Japan in 1975 and 1978, the battle to reduce the poisonous substances in exhaust fumes became extremely fierce among all manufacturers dealing with the relevant markets. Toyota refused to accept that exhaust purifying systems had to mean less efficient use of fuel, more noise, and higher production costs, and successfully developed

cars that meet the now even stricter international norms. At the beginning of the eighties the 30 millionth Toyota car came off the assembly line, to be followed only three years later, in 1983, by the 40 millionth. These figures make Toyota the biggest Japanese car producer, and the third biggest in the world. The turnover for 1984 was almost 5.5 billion yen (58% from car sales, 18% industrial vehicles, and the remaining 24% from other related and diverse interests), rising to 6.4 billion in the 1985 financial year. In 1985 Toyota had 8.8% penetration in the world car market. Production in 1980 was over 2,303,000, and in 1984, 2,413,000. To the latter figure should also be added the 139,000 (approx.) CKD units assembled in 29 Toyota plants in 20 different countries.

Meanwhile export figures for Toyota cars exceeded 1,100,000 in 1984 (not very different from the 1980 quota: growth here was held back by the self-regulating export policy with regard to Western markets agreed in common by all the Japanese car firms in the first half of the decade). Overall the most successful model on the overseas markets was the Corolla, of which almost 5.5 million were sold abroad between 1966 and 1984.

Corolla, Sprinter. The Corolla was updated again in 1974, though without major technical changes and retaining its 1.2-, 1.4- and 1.6-liter engines. New models were the hardtop and liftback, brought out in 1976 and 1977 respectively. With slight aesthetic alterations, the sedan, coupé, liftback and hardtop versions of the third generation Sprinter also came out now.

Cressida/Mk II/Chaser. The third generation Cressida or Mk II appeared in 1976 (left): 4-cylinder, 1,968 cc, or 6-cylinder 1,988 and 2,563 cc, the latter two being fitted on the Grande models. In 1977 a new version was offered (4-cylinder, 1,770 cc), and this was followed by a 2,188 cc diesel in 1979. The Chaser, brought out in 1977, was a particularly luxurious variant of the Mk II. Newly designed, but without major technical improvements, the fourth generation Cressida was brought out in 1980 (right).

Corona. In this generation of the Corona there were 74 different models, including the new five-door liftback sedan added alongside the traditional notchback version. The new engine on this occasion was a 1,840 cc (65 hp) diesel, with a maximum speed of 93 mph (150 km/h). Production of this series began in 1978.

Celica. A middle range sports model, the Celica (based on the Corona/Carina series) first appeared in 1970 as a coupé, then a few years later as a liftback (above). These two types of body were retained in the later ranges. The engines available were 4-cylinder, 1,588 and 1,968 cc, the latter incorporating electronic injection in 1974. The second generation appeared in August 1977 (below), with a 1,770 cc engine also available. A year later, the Celica Supra liftback model was fitted with a 6-cylinder electronic injection engine (2,563 cc, 140 hp).

Tercel/Corsa. The choice of middle range cars was expanded in 1978, when Toyota brought out its first front-wheel drive car, marketed as Tercel or Corsa. Available as notchback two- or four-door, or hatchback three- or five-door versions (left). Its engine was the same as that in the 1.3 and 1.5 liter Corolla. In 1982 the range was totally altered, with a four-wheel drive model also being introduced (above).

Exports to the United States topped 620,000 in 1985. Of these there were 168,000 Corollas and 128,000 Crowns. Of all cars produced, licensed, and exported in or from Japan, Toyotas represent about 30% in each case.

In 1982, with no more financial problems such as those that had led to the splitting of the company into Toyota Motor and Toyota Motor Sales in the fifties, production and marketing once again came to be handled by the same management.

Updating of the company's products was based on the work of three specialist research centers: the Toyota Central Research and Development Laboratories (concentrating on combustion, lubrication, new materials and new techniques of analysis), the Higashi-Fuji Technical Center (developing new technology for future application), and the Head Office Technical Center (where actual designs for market innovations are drawn). One of the more interesting developments in the eighties has been the electronic «TECS» (Total Engine Control System), introduced on regular models in 1980, which controls all the vital workings both of the engine and of the 4-shift automatic gears (worked previously by a hydraulic mechanism). During these years also numerous experimental prototypes were made to consolidate Toyota's technological efforts: worth mentioning are the EX-II (1981), the FX-1 (1983), and the FXV (1985) all featuring the very latest improvements of the day such as electronic-controlled suspension, four-wheel steering, full-time four-wheel drive, super/tur-

Camry/Vista. Further diversification of the middle range came in 1980, with the launching of the Camry/Vista models, developed from the Corona/Celica. There was a notchback four-door sedan and a five-door liftback. The earliest model (top) had a 4-cylinder engine (1.6-, 1.8-, or 2.0-liter). A new series, totally redesigned, with front-wheel drive, was introduced in 1983. Here are shown the two types of body (above and below). Partly the same as those in the Corona FF, the engines are all 4-cylinder, 1,832 cc (90 or 105 hp), 1,995 cc (107 or 120 hp), and 1,998 cc (160 hp, twin-camshaft, and 16 valves). On the diesel model the engine is a supercharged version (88 hp) of the 1,839 cc.

Corolla/Sprinter. The fourth generation Corolla/Sprinter appeared in 1979 with a series of modified engines from 1,290 cc (65 hp) and 1,588 cc (75, 86, or 108 hp), to a 1,770 cc (95 hp, reduced for the American market to 70 hp SAE). As an alternative there was also a 1,452 cc (80 hp) engine, adapted for various cars including the Sprinter illustrated here.

Celica. The third generation Celica came out in 1981, with a new range of engines, from 4-cylinder (1,587, 1,770, 1,832, and 1,972 cc) to 6-cylinder, 1,988 cc (125 hp basic model, 160 hp turbo with 24-valve model) and 2,759 cc (175 hp). Illustrated here are the Supra 2800 GT (above, left) and the 2000 GT (above, right). Launched at the 1985 Tokyo Motor Show, the fourth generation had front-wheel drive (illustrated below: the 2000 GT-R liftback, 4-cylinder, 2-liter, 150 hp, with 16 valves). The Celica is Toyota's second most successful export car after the Corolla.

Tercel/Sprinter Carib. Called either Tercel or Sprinter Carib, according to its intended market, this space-wagon with four-wheel drive, launched in 1981, has a 4-cylinder (1,452 cc) engine built in three versions; 71 hp for Europe, 83 hp for Japan, and 62 hp for the United States. The four-wheel drive can be engaged and disengaged. Some 212,000 of these had been built by 1984.

Corolla/Sprinter Trueno. The fifth generation Corolla appeared in 1983, in a vast range of models. Available bodies are the sedan (four-door notchback or five-door liftback) or a more compact hatchback model, the three- or five-door Corolla II. As well as these front-wheel drive models, there were the rear-wheel drive coupés (2- or 3-door) marketed as Corolla Levin and Sprinter Trueno (above). Left, the Corolla FX-GT.

Corona. In 1982 the seventh generation Corona appeared, at first (FR) with the traditional rear-wheel drive (above, left), then in 1983 with the option of a more modern front-wheel drive model (FF) with transverse engine (above, right), available also as liftback. Finally in the autumn of 1985 a front-wheel drive coupé was brought out (below), based on the new Celica, the GT-R version featuring a new 1,998 cc 16-valve engine (150 hp) with twin camshaft.

Hi-Lux. Most successful of a whole range of light commercial vehicles designed also for use as cars (especially for leisure driving), was the Hi-Lux. Based on Hino's Briska, it was launched in 1968 and marketed under the Toyota name after the takeover of Hino. Included in the range were the pick-up and station-wagon versions. Updated in 1972 (top, left), then again in 1978, the line retained gasoline engines (1.6- and 2-liter), though in 1979 a 2.2-liter diesel was also introduced. 1979 also saw the first four-wheel drive model, using the mechanical elements of the Land Cruiser. Here we see the 1980 Super de Lux (above, left) and the fourth generation 4WD: Surf Turbo SSR (top, right) and the Double Cab SR (above, right).

Crown. In 1983 the seventh generation of the Crown came out, of which on the left is the four-door hardtop version. The gasoline engines for these (all 6-cylinder) range from the 1,988 cc EFI (125 hp; available also in a turbo version, 145 hp, and with 4 valves per cylinder, 160 hp) to 2,954 cc (190 hp, also with 4 valves). A 4-cylinder diesel engine is also available (2,446 cc, 96 hp, or 105 hp turbo). During the 30 years of Crown production, a total of 2.8 million have been built.

Mk II/Chaser, Cresta. The fourth generation Mark II (above) came out in late 1984, combining ultra-modern four- or five-door body design with traditional rear-wheel drive. Engines: 4-cylinder, 1,832 cc (100 hp), 6-cylinder, 1,988 cc (130 hp basic model, 145 hp turbo with twin camshaft, 160 hp 4 valves per cylinder, and 185 hp turbo 24 valves), and supercharged 2,446 cc, 96 hp diesel. Slightly cheaper, the Cresta series (launched in 1980, below left) had the same engines as the Mk II, plus a diesel version (2.4-liter, 83 hp). As before, the Chaser (below, right) represents the most comprehensively equipped model. Overall between 1968 and 1984, over 3.7 million of these three models were built.

Starlet. The third generation Starlet appeared in 1984, the major innovation being front-wheel drive. Engines: 4-cylinder, 12 valves, 999 cc (54 hp, 93 mph, 150 km/h) and 1,295 cc (75 hp, 103 mph, 166 km/h carburetor version; 93 hp, 109 mph, 175 km/h electronic injection version).

MR-2. The MR-2, a two seater sportscar launched in 1984, has a central engine and comes in two versions: 1,452 cc (83 hp), and 16-valve 1,587 cc (130 or 124 hp according to whether or not the exhaust system with catalytic converter is fitted).

Carina. Based, mechanically, on the Corona, the Carina appeared in 1970, broadening the lower end of the Toyota middle range. The early lines were a two- (above) or four-door sedan, then a hardtop and station-wagon. In 1977 appeared the second series, slightly larger, with 1.4- and 2-liter engines. A further total restyling came with the third generation in 1981, of which the 1800 EFI 100 hp sedan is illustrated above, right. Along with this was the front-wheel drive Carina II (1983), developed at the same time as the Corona FF. A four-door hardtop version — stylistically and mechanically derived from the front-wheel drive Celica/Corona coupé — came out in August 1985. The version shown here (right) is the ED 2000G (2-liter, 16-valve, 150 hp). Production of the Carina between 1970 and 1984 was in the region of 2.3 million.

Soarer. The Soarer is a de luxe coupé based mechanically on the Mark II series, of which it retains the 8.7 ft (2,660 mm) wheelbase among other things. Brought out in 1981, it has two 6-cylinder engines: 1,988 cc (electronic injection, 130 hp basic model; 24 valves, 160 hp) and 2,954 cc, also with 4 valves per cylinder, 190 hp (brought out in 1985, replacing a similar 2,759 cc model).

Land Cruiser. More than 1.5 million Land Cruisers were made between its launch and the end of 1985. Almost 95% have been for exports, all around the globe, and these figures speak for themselves regarding the success of this model. Brought out in February 1951, the earliest version, the 3.4-liter, 6-cylinder BJ, was built exclusively to order until 1953. Regular production only really started the following year, with the Land Cruiser. In 1956 a 3.9-liter gasoline engine was fitted, and this was not replaced until 1975 (with a more powerful 4.2 liter version). A diesel engine (3.6 liter) was once again made available in 1972 (adapted to 3-liter two years afterwards, then 3.2 and eventually 3.4). Offering three different wheelbases and body designs (a canvas roof model was introduced alongside the five-door station-wagon and the hardtop in 1967), the Land Cruiser (station-wagon) was radically restyled in 1980 (below, left), and a new series of bodies was brought out (hardtop, station-wagon and canvas top above). The engines were 4-cylinder diesel (2.4- and 3.4-liter) and a 6-cylinder 4-liter gasoline model (between 72 and 155 hp). Four-wheel drive (rear or front and rear). Five-speed with transfer box. Below, right the Land Cruiser wagon 70S of 1985. In partnership with the Portuguese firm «Caetano Sarl,» production of a 5-cylinder, 2.5 turbodiesel (made by the Italian company V.M., and intended for the European market) started at Porto in 1986. Meanwhile «Toyota do Brasil» is manufacturing the Bandeirante, using the old body and a 4-cylinder, 3.8-liter Mercedes diesel engine.

bocharger system, engines running on partially lean mixtures, as well as aerodynamic design improvements and increased passenger comfort.

Toyota's technical and commercial aggressiveness had led to more lively international contacts, and negotiation of a number of collaboration agreements. Undoubledly the most significant of these was the ten-year contract agreed in February 1983 with General Motors, which led to the creation of the New United Motor Manufacturing Inc. (NUMMI) for production at the General Motors factory in Fremont (California), under Toyota technical direction, of a model based on the Japanese Sprinter and marketed as Chevrolet Nova. The first of this line left the factory in December 1984. Both sides had their own reasons for this collaboration. G.M. will, by the expiry of the contract, have sufficient know-how to develop and produce the future generation of the Nova itself; while Toyota, who invested some 600 million dollars in this joint venture, and who will receive 2.5% royalties from its American part-

ner, was enabled to enter the American sector with a smaller margin of risk. Production capacity is 200,000 per annum.

The importance of the North American market for Toyota is also apparent from the fact that it now has its own factory in Kentucky, which will produce some 200,000 cars a year as from 1988, and an assembly plant in Canada intended to bring out 50,000 p.a. again from 1988.

Toyota's European interests are a shareholding in Lotus (1985) the biggest British sportscar manufacturer, acquired by G.M. in 1986.

The Toyota group in the eighties consists of 13 main companies, of which the Toyota Motor Co. is the principal one. Along with these are affiliated firms (Hino and Daihatsu) and a further thousand or so small and medium sized businesses, all under the giant's umbrella. The group does not only produce cars; prefabricated houses are another of its concerns, as well as those other sectors already mentioned.

Blizzard. Developed in 1980 from the Daihatsu Taft, the off-road Blizzard (2.2-liter diesel, 72 hp) was totally redesigned in 1984 (above). New engines were also introduced: 2,446 cc 83 hp and 96 hp turbo, both diesel. The chassis has box-type ladder frame with front and rear rigid axle. Four-wheel drive, and 5-speed automatic transmission with transfer-box. Maximum road speed 81 mph (130 km/h).

Century. Only slightly modified since its launch in 1967, the Century sedan is the company's prestige car. Originally V8 cylinders, 2,981 cc, 150 hp, the engine was raised in 1973 to 3,376 cc, 180 hp. The following year transistorized ignition was fitted. Then finally in 1982 a new V8 3,994 cc (190 hp) engine was introduced. Pneumatic suspension was brought in 1985. The Century is 17 ft (5.12 m) long and weights 3,924 lb (1,780 kg). Illustrated here is the 1986 version.

Ace. In 1984 Toyota production of commercial vehicles topped one million, representing 23% of all Japanese production in this area. Among these was the Ace «wagon» series, first brought out in 1967, which is very close in concept to the space-wagon car. The line expanded steadily in three parallel ranges: the initial Hi-Ace, the small Lite-Ace (1970) and the Master-/Town-Ace (1976). Here we see examples of each range: the 1980 Lite-Ace wagon (left), the Master-Ace (right) with four-wheel drive and 2-liter turbodiesel engine (1985), and the 2400 turbodiesel Hi-Ace (1985, below).

GENERAL INDEX

Numbers in bold refer to illustrations